RIDING THE MILKWAY

Babette Gallard

This book is dedicated to my Father

The author gratefully acknowledges the help of Catherine (Cat) Sharman who drove the second horse trailer down to our starting point at Le Puy en Velay; Edward Stankard who helped us in too many ways to list here, but without whom life would have been a great deal more complicated; Raymond Gallard for his contribution at the start, middle and end of the road; Lucy

Gallard for her artistic contributions to this book, participation in the pilgrimage itself and of course for being our wonderful daughter; then finally one huge, all-encompassing bellow of thanks goes to the villagers of St Aubin Fosse Louvain who supported us every step of the way and continue to treat our horses like the celebrities they are.

© Babette Gallard

First edition, April 2004

All rights reserved. No part of the publication may be reproduced, stored in a retrieval system or transmitted in any form by any means, electronic, mechanical photocopying, and recording or otherwise except brief extracts for the purpose of a review, without permission of the publisher and copyright owner.

THE ROAD TO THE STARS

PREPARATION

  BABETTE - WHY HORSES?

  PAUL - WHY SANTIAGO?

INTRODUCING THE TEAM

  PROGRESS

  TRIAL RUN

PAUL - ON VERTIGO

　　NO TURNING BACK

FRENCH SECTION (CHEMIN DU PUY): LE PUY EN VELAY TO THE PYRENEES

　　CONGENITALLY CLUMSY FRENCH TROTTER

　　HOUDINI

　　WHO FORGOT TO TELL FRANCE IT WAS SUMMER?

　　…AND HE RESTED ON THE SEVENTH DAY (GEN. 2:2-3)

　　FRUSTRATION! IMPATIENCE!

　　BAGS OF PASTA

　　CONQUES – WHERE IT ALL STARTED

　　ANGELS

　　AN OCEAN OF STONES

　　MISUNDERSTOOD TEENAGER

　　ROCK FACES AND BALLET SHOES

　　HELLO AND GOODBYE

　　PILGRIMS

　　FUR, FEATHER AND WINGS

　　ANOTHER ST. JAMES VICTIM

　　INCLEMENT WEATHER

　　<u>VANDALS</u>

　　<u>LAND OF THE LIVING</u>

　　AN ATTACK OF BUCOLIA

　　FOOTHILLS OF THE PYRENEES

　　LUCY

　　AND ONWARDS

SPANISH SECTION (EL *CAMINO* FRANCES):

RONCEVALLES TO SANTIAGO DE COMPOSTELA

FEEDING SPANISH STYLE

DRAWBRIDGES AND DRAWBACKS

SAINTS AND ANGELS

ON FOOT - IN ESPADRILLES

ES MUY BUEN

DONATIVOS

PAUL – ONE THOUSAND KILOMETRES

BURGOS

OASIS

MESETA BLUES

PILGRIMS FROM HELL

MORE ANGELS

BIRTHDAY

GOODBYE MESETA. GOODBYE N120

HEADING FOR THE HILLS

HONEY, GOLD AND SILVER

LAND OF CONTRASTS

  PAUL

  PIGS WITH WINGS

  WHO LEFT THE HEAVENLY HOSE ON?

  THANK YOU BERNARD

EPILOGUE

  NO EUPHORIA HERE PLEASE

  FOOTNOTES

THE ITINERARY

Babette Gallard

THE ROAD TO THE STARS

Pilgrims have been making their way to Santiago de Compostela since the 12th century, starting out from all corners of the earth and converging on a route that traces the path of the Milky Way, east to west, through Santiago de Compostela and into the sea at Finisterre – earth's end.

The route was long, arduous and often very dangerous, but pilgrims kept coming in their thousands. For some, the motivation would have been entirely religious, but for many others it was far more basic and earthly. The sick hoped St James would cure their bodily ills. Criminals chose the long haul in preference to a prison sentence imposed by a court of law, while a large percentage of the other pilgrims would have been aiming to enhance their credibility and social status back home by displaying the St James cockle shell as proof of their grit and devotion.

Today's pilgrims do not experience anything approaching the same degree of physical hardship, though they still have just as many diverse or sometimes weird reasons for putting themselves on the road to Santiago, a category Paul and I have probably been consigned to by most of our friends. Our motivation came from a pair of dreams and a series of coincidences that somehow merged and became our seventy-five day, sixteen-hundred-kilometre-long horse ride from Le Puy en Velay in

France to Santiago de Compostela in Spain - a journey of discovery in every sense of the word.

During our preparations, both practical and spiritual, we researched the subject of St James himself and found the smattering of history and myth that together create the Apostle, whose supposed remains thousands of pilgrims visit every year. From this we learnt that it is in fact extremely doubtful that he ever visited Spain and reports of St. James the Moor slayer (Santiago Matomoro) appearing on a white horse in 844 AD were created by hired storytellers. Even the idea that his relics were finally transported to Iberia was probably just a fabrication of the Church.

Some people may find this obvious deceit rather shocking, but it is a well-authenticated historical fact that many of the founding legends of medieval pilgrimage shrines were nothing more than tall tales conjured up by enterprising church administrators. Quite sensibly, they recognized that the number of pilgrims visiting and donating money to a shrine was proportional to the miraculous nature of the founding legend, and nothing has changed in this respect.

Travelling today on the St. James Way is still a commercial affair. Pilgrims bring much needed revenue and the route is sometimes diverted to take in villages and towns to maximise these opportunities.

The flip-side is that in return pilgrims can enjoy facilities that make the difference between unacceptable hardship and an accessible experience for people of any age and fitness.

Paul and I chose to ride our road to the stars on horseback, just as Aimery Picaud (author of the Liber Sancti Jacobi and first guidebook writer for the St. James Way) and his even more affluent and influential contemporaries did, but this is where the similarities stop. Neither affluent nor influential, we are two very ordinary people who managed to fulfil a dream by pooling our meagre resources, putting ourselves at the mercy of the

Milky Way and seeing how far our three horses and dog were prepared to take us.

Before leaving we did our best to fit in with the pilgrim mode by putting our affairs into order and detaching ourselves from the trappings of petty materialism that surrounded us, though we drew the line at wearing sack cloth and carrying a gourd.

Of course the reality was that daily encounters with so many people and the ego-thrill of being asked where we were going and how far we had been, overtook the majority of our best intentions, but three months on and with sufficient distance between then and now, I can sincerely say that our direction and focus in specific aspects of our lives have changed, and I hope for the better. How and how much better only you the reader can judge, but above all we hope that you enjoy our story and are able to appreciate the role played by our wonderful horses that turned our dreams into reality.

BABETTE - WHY HORSES?

My relationship with equines is fairly complicated. In one context I have spent a large portion of my life trying to avoid the beasts, while in another I have an idyllic image of being with them day in, day out. I blame my mother for both viewpoints.

It all started with a basket saddle, or to be more precise, a photograph of me wedged into one, with my proud father standing to one side. Cute perhaps, but off-scene my ambitious mother has already decided to complete the illusion by sending me to a boarding school filled with nuns, children called Belinda and ponies.

Apparently some parents think ponies are a developmental necessity for their children, but it's all wasted on me because I'm petrified of them and resent being dumped into stinging nettles. I try to say so, but unfortunately I'm better in the saddle than the classroom, and someone tells my mother that I'm really quite a capable little rider. Actually, I've just perfected the art of jabbing my heels into the pony's sides to avoid being thrown off, but no one seems to notice and anyway it doesn't matter because in my absence Mother has been adding to her own equine collection at home. Horses are to be indelibly etched into my future whether I like it or not. In the winter holidays I have to go hunting and in the summer it's the shows. As the years go by the mounts get bigger and more dangerous, but I somehow manage to survive - a mistake on my part.

Next, my mother discovers eventing, or in other words jumping over wooden fences that don't give way when you, your horse or both together fall on them. A painful process for those concerned, but exciting and uncharted territory for a Polish immigrant desperate to climb the English social ladder. Time to cut the long-story short. By sixteen I am an accomplished, if reluctant rider. I have competed in big name places, done inexplicably well and have all the kit to go with my status: a horsebox, a groom, a vile attitude and unbeknownst to anyone else, a phobia. I am terrified. I'd rather throw myself off the horse than go over a jump with it, but paradoxically riding has also become my identity and unfortunately I adore Mick McGilligan, my 15 hands high, Connemara Thoroughbred cross. Mick and I are mates, we understand our fears and we go places for each other, but then a strange combination of accidents changes everything: my life, my mother's aspirations and my horses.

Summer of 1970. 'O' levels and what should have been a revision period in the library, but I'm not interested because I hate school and refuse to conform. On this particular day I abscond completely, disappearing into a small attic space above the school hall where it's quiet and no one can find me. I take a book, because I am a great reader, but when I get there I find something even more interesting: our present History teacher's name scrawled up in chalk presumably when she was (inconceivably) a teenager like me.

Ruth Cook 1958.

Perhaps it is a lure, because the floor is certainly a trap; painted glass that shatters and leaves me to fall 20 metres onto the wooden hall floor below. Result: a broken neck, four crushed lumber vertebrae, cracked skull and numerous other injuries that heal unnoticed beside the more spectacular ones. As a consequence, I languish in plaster for a few weeks, read a book my mother has dug up from an old pile at home and meet my hero, Alan Marshall.

Alan was an Australian who, in spite of being on crutches as a result of polio, takes two horses, a completely unsuitable caravan and his citified wife, round the Australian outback during the Second World War. His aim is to collect messages for the boys who are fighting for the so-called motherland, but for me his book achieves far more. His refusal to accept the limitations of his physical disability enabled me to overcome mine. His relationship with his horses highlighted the very real value of my own tenuous link with Mick, and in spite of coming from another world and time, the people he described came alive for me then, and resonate still. In short, Alan Marshall lived my dream and I've been dreaming of living his ever since.

After this fairly traumatic episode, all goes well for a respectable number of years. My mother loses interest in me and I am able to, almost, forget about riding, but the great horse in the sky is only biding his time until I have my own daughter in idyllic rural surroundings, which suddenly seem strangely empty without the obligatory pony. I repeat history, but I hope without the pressure. Lucy is as nervous as I was and I allow her to be. We dabble for a while until I start working abroad, and anything more than her by now ageing pony becomes out of the question. Once again, equines disappear from my life, until I leave my husband and meet Paul.

Paul is eminently sensible, but has an unnerving habit of taking my wildest ideas and turning them into reality. Three years into the relationship and you'd think he'd know better, but it seems that in this respect he's just not willing to learn. I blame our holiday in the south of France for our latest folly; the sun must have fried my brains.

Me: 'I've always fancied buying a Camargue horse and riding back home.'

Paul: 'Sounds good to me. When shall we set off?'

So here we are, some of the practicalities dealt with, because I have taken redundancy and Paul early retirement, meaning we have the time, if not the money, to do what we want. We are living in France too, which would have cut the trip down if Paul hadn't added his own component to the plan: the St. James Way to Santiago de Compostela in Spain. The idea of using Camargue ponies does survive for a while, at least until we speak to some of the breeders and find out how much a useful specimen is likely to cost. So now all that remains of my original proposal is the word horse and nothing on earth will remove that, as I know only too well.

PAUL - WHY SANTIAGO?

Having thus lost his understanding, he unluckily stumbled upon the oddest fantasy that ever entered into a madman's brain.
Don Quixote

We were on a meandering course from our home in Northern France to a walking holiday in the Picos de Europa in Spain. There was Babette, Lucy, four-month-old Vasco (the dog) and me. Babette had fallen in love with the Picos years before, and this was her opportunity to show them off to Lucy and the new man in her life, me. The meandering was a definite plot on my part, because after months of toil in renovating our farmhouse through all weathers, I was going to make the holiday last and enjoy every kilometre of the journey.

My course, if that is how you describe pointing the car at the midday sun, had brought us eventually to the medieval town of Conques and one of those warm, misty French mornings when the world seems to be perfect. It is still early and the town is deserted as we climb the cobbled streets from our riverside camp. The routes in and out of Conques are sufficiently slow and winding to discourage the tourists until late morning, and so we have the town to ourselves. I try to explain the little that I can remember about the pilgrim roads to Santiago de Compostela, and the roles of the abbeys such as Ste. Foy in providing sanctuary for the pilgrims.

As we tour the cloisters of the abbey and gaze across the steep and misted river valley to a chapel high above wooded hills, it is easy to cut the ties with the frenetic world in which we have spent our working lives. But, whoa, what is that strange feeling? Vertigo? If we put ourselves in the position of those pilgrims thousands of years earlier, without the pressures of our careers, the futures of our mutually acquired children or even the house renovation, what would happen inside these heads of ours? I truly did not know.

Neither Babette nor I have any recognisable religion. Neither can we conceive of the existence of any omnipotent power, even though we do both wear our post-hippie morals on our sleeves and each have our own, often strongly expressed, views of what is fair or right. So, as pilgrims we could not expect the road to lead us to Damascus, but if not there, then where?

While these fairly imprecise questions exercise my mind, our exploration of Conques leads us across a narrow Roman river bridge and beside a pasture in which two white horses are grazing. The conversation turns to recollections of Robin Hanbury-Tenison's book on his travels through France on two white Camargue horses. Then, as we return to the abbey of Ste. Foy and the centre of the village, we encounter a couple hiking the opposite way, each sporting the pilgrim's Saint James cockle shell.

Babette has described me as sensible, others see me as hopelessly romantic and impractical, while most also know me as determined, or perhaps the more appropriate word is obstinate. Well, you must judge which, but one *café noir* later we have decided that our next summer will be spent following the entire length of the St. James Way from Le Puy en Velay to Santiago de Compostela, on horseback. Of course, when a decision is made there is no going back, even though there are a few details that we need to work on: I cannot ride, we have no horses and early retirement, house building and marriage break-ups have left us skint.

I grew up as an only and adopted child of a poor and frequently unhappy couple. My mum was vocal in bemoaning her lot, while my dad's frustrations were hidden behind a violent temper, though never directed towards me. I had few friends and so escaped the conflict of the household into the world of the dreams that I could create in my head. We had no books in the house, but the cinema, radio and black and white TV fed my phantasies. The radio dial was an atlas of romantic names; Reykjavik, Rabat, Luxembourg, Cairo, Moscow. I would construct elaborate aerials and lie with my ear pressed to the speaker, minutely adjusting the tuning dial, hoping to separate an intelligible voice from the whistles and crosstalk, enthralled when I heard "It's midnight in Europe and this is the American Forces Network".

Education was very much a two-part affair: ten years of confusion and embarrassment heading towards a boiler suit, and the role of long term bread winner for my parents, then a flashbulb recognition that this need not be the way and seven years of graft to a maths degree. After that, career planning was straightforward, the highest salary on offer and as much travel as I could get, which brings me to the place you find me now thirty-five years, two marriages, two careers and five continents later, on a horse with a bad case of vertigo.

INTRODUCING THE TEAM

Ah that horse! How we loved her! She had front teeth like a row of shovels in a shop window. Her pendulous underlip drooped like an open purse ... Her apparently dejected air was a manifestation of piety rather than pessimism ... but Millie was always willing to co-operate.
From These Are My People, by Alan Marshall

When I look at my diary now, I see that it is only three months since we really started to turn our mad dream into reality by beginning the search for our horses. Having rejected the idea of buying Camargue ponies, our criteria were adjusted to include any equine over 13hh, no younger than four, no further than 100 kilometres away and no more than 1000 Euros. Surely there had to be three horses that could fall into this very broad category.

Horse trading in rural France is different from anything I have ever experienced before. We bought Okapi on the seventh of February this year (2005), though it is hard to remember the precise details, because we were all very drunk at the time. Christian, our good friend and expert Percheron breeder, had taken it on himself to find the right horse for us, which involved visiting just about every farm in the vicinity, where everyone knew him and everyone had an open bottle of Calvados.

Okapi was number four on the list to view and not the most prepossessing, but he was solid and well balanced from what I could see, though even the best horse would have found it hard to show off his paces in knee deep mud and slurry. I sucked my teeth and tried not to sway. He had a kind eye, I felt sorry for him and he was ludicrously cheap. The boy was coming home.

Gwendolyn (originally called Krisma) followed shortly after, once again through a contact of Christian's, though this time I was sober enough to look at her more closely and demand a month's trial before making a decision. After all, she was little better than wild, very hairy and very ugly, but she reminded me of how I imagine Alan Marshall's Millie to have been, so our fates were already sealed.

Lubie came last, almost as an afterthought, because I was still wavering between having two horses or three. Did we need a pack pony or not? She was tied to a tree when we saw her, failure written all over her face and scars etched on her legs. The perfect misfit to add to our motley crew.

At this point it is probably time to provide more detailed biographies for the members of our fairly unimpressive team.

First, and only because I'm the primary narrator, I will start with myself. A forty-seven-year-old phobic rider, reasonably fit but never sporty, able to camp, but unable to sleep on anything less than a well pumped airbed, in need of at least two showers a day and positively pathological about clean underwear.

Attributes: a working knowledge of horses and not a lot else.

Predicted problems: Tendency to despair and impatience.

Paul, exactly ten years older, awesomely intelligent, exasperatingly sporty, happy to pitch a tent in any country and plunge into any language (even when he can't speak a word), tolerant and where I am concerned utterly gullible.

Attributes: skilled reader of maps, resourceful and courageous.

Predicted problems: At the time of writing Paul has ridden for a total of two weeks, has only limited experience of being with horses and has just broken his arm after his first fall ever (Okapi bucked and I don't know who was the more surprised, horse or rider, when Paul landed head first on the verge).

Gwendolyn (Gwen), a 16hh, seven-year-old mare of unknown breed, deemed unrideable as a five-year-old and discarded to repent her sins in a sparse field ever since. A well-proportioned horse if looked at in sections, but a bizarre misfit when taken as a whole. Her head is coffin shaped, but her heart is pure gold, if she likes you. If not, stand clear. It took five weeks to get on her, which involved experiences similar to sitting on an unexploded bomb and refusals to move in any direction whatsoever.

Purchase price: 450 Euros

Attributes: An intermittent desire to please that comes into its own when most needed. Asked nicely, Gwen will pass anything and set an example to her less courageous companions. She is also a natural nanny for the other two, alerting us immediately if anything is untoward or someone is misbehaving.

Predicted problems: Weight loss and a potentially weak back, which I suspect comes from a previous injury – she has a tendency to throw herself to the ground if crossed. Gwen was little more than a skeleton when she came to us, riddled with worms and unable fully to digest the high-value food we gave her. Her back seems to be gaining in strength which makes her marginally more comfortable to ride, but after eight weeks of feeding she is still underweight.

Okapi – our pack pony. An unbroken, but very good-looking, 13hh rising four year old [1]Poney Francais de Selle gelding. We were able to ride him in the same time span as Gwen, but he would probably have been amenable to the prospect sooner. The boy is basically sweet-natured, but has an inbuilt inferiority complex after a lifetime of living with six towering [2]

Percherons. As a result, he feels the need to prove himself on occasion.

Purchase price: 600 Euros

Attributes: Ability to get fat on air. Within a week of arriving as an undernourished waif, his stomach was barely clearing the ground. Sturdiness, he is an ideal pack pony, but well able to carry us too.

Predicted problems: teenage tantrums and fitness. Okapi is as fat as a barrel, lazy and still relatively young for hard work.

Lubie (meaning whim in French – how appropriate) our only broken horse, a six-year-old trotter mare, too slow for the race track and too tough for the dinner plate. I felt sorry for her, she looked all right and we didn't have the time or the money to waste scouring the country for something better, so we bought her and hoped for the best. I have no regrets.

Purchase price: 900 Euros.

Attributes: A keen, but safe mount for Paul, well used to traffic, barking dogs and all the usual horse hazards.

Predicted problems: Weight loss and general fitness. Trotters are used to high octane fuel. Past and as yet undiscovered injuries may also take their toll.

Kim was at the waddly, carry-your-socks-away stage when we first met him, but as he grew our doubts did likewise. Kim developed bow legs like a miniature bulldog. He was black and tan and swept away to a rear that was as impudent as his temperament.

From These Are My People, by Alan Marshall

Vasco (Vasco), our beloved, sort of fox terrier, bought in a

French market a year ago for no reason other than that we felt sorry for him. A loyal, bottomless pit of energy who has taken to riding in a big way.

Purchase Price: No idea

Attributes: Everything that is Vasco

Predicted problems: cars and cows. He forgets the existence of the former and chases the latter.

Now for the practicalities, at least on the horse front, because the rest is left to Paul who is eminently more practical than I am. In the relatively short time we have spent in preparation, I have seen that long distance riding is completely different from anything I have ever done before. I consider myself to be a reasonably experienced horsewoman, but I've had to learn all over again, which requires some humility.

Tack? What kind of tack?

Feed? How much? Where from?

Shoes? Farriers? Good? Bad? Cost?

Question after question, but nothing in my past experience pointing to the answers, because I've come from the relatively rarefied world of eventing and latterly dressage.

In my quest for information I have read numerous books and consulted the excellent Long Riders Guild website, which has made me realise that our trip is a mere, proverbial stone's throw for real Distance Riders. I have resisted the temptation to give up before even starting and have read every account, only to find that there are as many views as the people who give them. The advice ranges from nothing but the rough-it way, to carrying a lap top and travelling with a team of horses. But who is right? Well of course it all depends on the aims and circumstances and I have to find my level somewhere between the two. Paul and I are working to a fixed budget. We cannot afford a back-up team to carry feed, identify campsites or transport equipment, so as a minimum we have to be able to carry all that we need and know how we are going to deal with the question of feed and hooves on route. A tall order.

To date I have opted for equipment that is both light and cheap, so synthetic materials feature (I can hear my father turning somersaults in his grave). Our horses are ridden in a very mild form of bitless bridle, because after the rigours of dressage riding I prefer neck-reining, which comes with the added advantage that the horses will be able to graze without the restriction of a bit in their mouths.

All our horses are being trained to respond to the voice as much as to the customary rein and leg aids, a useful addition, but also fundamental in view of Paul's inexperience. If nothing else, either he or I can bellow 'Stand!' if anything should go wrong. A few practice runs have been reasonably successful. Vasco is also included in this programme, and now understands the command *Hold*, which means he should take a trailing rope and lead the horse. Fine until he gets bored and decides to investigate a rabbit hole instead - Gwen simply refuses to play the game.

Perhaps the most courageous/foolish decision (only time will tell) I have made is to use plastic boots as opposed to metal shoes. I have long been a proponent of barefoot riding and find it slightly galling that all the big names are now recommending it, when twenty years ago my horsy colleagues were consigning me to the hippy-bin for advocating just the same. The use of metal shoes for a ride of 1600 kilometres raises all sorts of issues. First the location of the farriers and then their skill - bad workmanship can cripple a horse - but perhaps even more seriously the problems caused by nail holes in hooves that will need reshoeing at least every three or four weeks. Hooves are not pin cushions and with a horse like Gwen, who has particularly poor feet as a result of her previous malnutrition, the results can be catastrophic. So plastic it is and wherever possible and for as long as possible, barefoot.

Progress

With five weeks to go we are all getting fitter and after some initial problems, I think the boots will work. How easy that single sentence makes it all sound. What about the sleepless nights spent worrying about Gwen's flat heels that no boot could possibly hang on to? If she were a human she would be wearing orthopaedic shoes. And what about the weeks of solid rain that turned our fields into a swamp and rotted Lubie's hooves? What about Gwen's sunburnt nose …. but I haven't the time and you as the reader surely won't have the patience to listen to me whingeing about what is already history, well some of it – the skin on Gwen's nose is still peeling off in sheets as I write. BUT we have hit the 15 kilometre distance mark without any sign of fatigue – equine or human (we hope to achieve an average of 26 kilometres per day). We have negotiated some of the worst terrain imaginable: rocks, mud, low trees, thunder storms and horror of horrors (in Lubie's case) running water. The equipment is holding out well, the boots are beginning to fit and stay on without rubbing. Gwen is putting on weight and on occasion moving like a horse instead of a camel. Okapi's teenage tantrums have been replaced by enthusiasm and Paul has managed to persuade Lubie that not every trot is a race. We are making progress.

Good news on the transport too. Quite by coincidence we have met a wonderful woman called Catherine (Cat) who originally came to collect some manure, but went away with something she says is much more exciting: the prospect of towing a second trailer down to Le Puy en Velay and collecting us latterly in Spain. Then, after letting me show off some of my horsy knowledge for a few minutes, she announced that in England she had been a Show Judge for Mountain and Moorland ponies. What a find!

Less satisfyingly, we are still waiting for our pack saddle to arrive from Canada, without which we can't really test the total weight of what we hope to take and whether Okapi is able to carry it. Worse still, this means that we will have to delay our trial trip, something we really must do before we leave in order to find out if there are any weaknesses or gaps in our equipment. We already know that the amazing two-second-tent, so-called because it only takes this time to erect, takes two hours to get back in the bag. I have visions of it unfolding whilst on Okapi's back and launching him skywards like a huge kite.

Meanwhile, both Gwen and Lubie have decided to have teeth problems, spitting out great green blobs of half chewed grass, so that I am in no doubt that something has to be done – more expense. Then, as if that wasn't bad enough, Lubie's foot rot is showing worrying signs of turning into a large hole in the most sensitive area of her hoof – the frog. I will have to get the farrier over, something I know I should have done a while ago, but have avoided because of the comments I will have to endure with regard to the boots. I won't tell him about them, but he will find out and shake his doleful head at the stupidity of women and in particular English women, though I should be used to it by now.

To add to all of this, as if we didn't have enough to worry about, we are also frantically planning a barbecue as a way of thanking everyone in the village and beyond for all their support. It has to be done; everyone has taken such an interest, keeping their dogs at bay and slowing down tractors and cars when passing a horse performing somersaults on the side of the road. Just one problem. I can't cook. Point to Mount Everest and I will try to climb it, but ask me to prepare a salad in the kitchen and I dissolve into tears. That's why my first question to all of my long-term partners (three) has been do you cook? Paul does, but not for fifty people.

But let's look on the bright side. In spite of the weather and our own inadequacies we are making progress. Okapi is leading well from Gwen and we have managed another 15 kilometres through some very uncomfortable terrain, with only the weather preventing us from doing another 10 kilometres with ease. The one problem we did have was a broken strap on one of Lubie's boots, clearly a weakness in the system, but better found out here than somewhere out there.

Two days ago the cow bells arrived from my brother in Switzerland, but the idea of using them came from one of the many long distance riding accounts I have been reading. They are a good way of tracking your horses when, as is inevitable, they decide that the grass is definitely greener somewhere a long way from your tent. We attached the bells to the head collars of Okapi and Lubie without incident, but of course Gwen had to make a fuss and spent the next half hour racing up and down the field in an attempt to run away from the clanging monster dangling from her chin. It was a predictably hysterical response, though I have to say that after two days of the infernal row I can sympathise with her objections.

We have also survived the farrier, who was embarrassingly compliant and eager to assist us in any way he could, particularly with respect to preparing some extra shoes for us to take in addition to the first set he wanted to put on a week prior to departure. I didn't have the courage to admit that we were using the boots and thanked him with a dishonest promise to get in touch nearer the time. If I'd been made of wood the blackbirds would have been nesting on my elongated nose in their thousands. He then went on to comment on Gwen's rather singular appearance, saying that her size and shape of head were proof positive that she came from traditional French Trotter stock. This could also be an explanation for the sorry state in which we found her, because even in her most willing and attentive moments Gwen trips over her own shadow, so the thought of her careering headlong down a race track with all four legs completely out of control is terrifying. No one in their right mind would have considered her for the job. But on the positive side, he pronounced their hooves to be in generally good condition, which would seem to indicate that the vastly expensive potions we have been plastering on them must have done some good.

Now, with just under four weeks to go it is time to take stock of our readiness and ability to achieve our aims. When I look out of the window today, I can see our three horses grazing quietly in the field below and on the face of it they appear to be relatively fit and able. Gwen is positively sleek and her rump almost rounded, while all of them are showing distinct signs of musculature. But, and there is always a but, it all depends on the context. They are admirably suited to riding out along the gentle country lanes and farm tracks of the region where we live (Mayenne) and positively enjoy it, even Gwen. Paul is becoming increasingly competent with Lubie and together they have already tackled some quite serious terrain that would challenge far more experienced riders and horses. But is that enough?

There are some fundamental weaknesses in our plans that leap out at me before even beginning to examine the situation in any detail. Other than Okapi, the horses we have chosen are completely unsuited to the task we have set them. Gwen is a large horse, clumsy as an arthritic camel and about as comfortable. I am the only one who can safely ride her and the food still goes in one end and comes out undigested from the other – muesli poos as Paul calls them. Lubie is a race horse and though apparently impossible to tire, is nevertheless unused to conserving her energy over long distances. Okapi, our pack pony, is physically capable of carrying the weight, but is young and has shown sensitivity to anything that rattles or touches his rump. And that's just the horses. What about the humans? So far my only physical issue has been the wearing of thongs over long distances – not a good idea – but I expect my legs will suffer a degree of wear and tear that even our fancy new full [3]chaps won't prevent. More worryingly, Paul is showing signs of back pain, a symptom of an old ailment that I am saying needs to be addressed now by visiting a chiropractor. He is not keen but sees the sense of avoiding serious pain and possible inability to ride at all.

Then there is the timescale of the whole expedition. Nothing in our lives can happen in isolation and there are a number of factors we have to consider in relation to my daughter Lucy. Our leaving date has now, finally, been set for the 29th of June. Why? Because she finishes her Brevet (the equivalent of the English G.C.S.E's) on the 28th and there is no way we are leaving before the exams are out of the way. After that she will spend the summer with Ray, her father, and hopefully squeeze in a week or two with us. But in September she starts at the Lycée (equivalent of 6th form college) in Laval, a town some forty minutes' drive from here, where she will be boarding during the week. Once again, we have to be there to ensure that she is settled in and happy. Hence the very clear target of 26 kilometres per day, with rest periods in between. But is it wise to impose such a stark regime on ourselves and the horses on our first very trip? Absolutely not!

And finally there is the farewell barbecue, rather like the headline wedding before the headline divorce, or perhaps I'm just allowing my fears to take me one step too far. I have visions of us returning, tails literally between our legs, having failed within the first two weeks. Or worse still, refusing to admit failure by hiring transport and constructing scenes of us riding along idyllic tracks. Anyway, the invitations are going out regardless, and the number of attendees is possibly increasing, though we have no gauge and are bound to get it wrong whichever side of caution we take. More than fifty? Less than fifty? And as if that weren't stressful enough, our tight schedule has forced us to opt for the 25th of June, my birthday when I will be forty-seven and look every day of sixty.

TRIAL RUN

Isn't it wonderful when things go according to plan or possibly even better? We have just returned from an almost entirely successful trial run and I, the eternal pessimist am, for once, entirely optimistic.

With the leaving date drawing ever closer and our pack saddle still somewhere on a ship between Canada and France, we have been getting increasingly worried about the need to test ourselves and the equipment. Then one evening Paul suggests that we turn my father's old cavalry saddle into a temporary pack saddle. I am initially sceptical, but on closer examination I can see that he is right, because the family heirloom is perfectly balanced and festooned with metal rings designed for attaching various kinds of kit. Ten minutes later, Paul has tied our rucksacks, one on either side of the saddle, and after that it is simply a matter of putting it on Okapi.

I'll admit it now, I held my breath and hoped for the best. Okapi has accepted a lightweight saddle, and with some minor opposition the special pad we have bought for the pack, but how would he view the contraption that Paul and I were about to lower on to his back?

We plonk a large bowl of feed in front of him, and advance from behind, the saddle held aloft. My heart stops as we lower it … and then … nothing, not even a shudder. The little chap continues eating as if this is the kind of thing humans do all the time. So from there it is all systems go. Paul finds a place to ride to and a place to stay. We tell ourselves that testing a campsite would be better, but are quietly relieved when only an *auberge* is available – hot baths and a good meal are hard to resist.

We set off in the morning, a ride of some 27 kilometres ahead and the sun in the sky. Paul, the most accomplished map reader in the world as far as I am concerned, has put together a route that combines some road work with a great deal more off-road [4]*grande randonnee* tracks between farms and fields – the perfect combination.

Four hours in and still no mishaps. The horses are fit and our spirits high. I begin to appreciate the value of travelling distances slowly, and note that even cows have different expressions and natures. It's cliché stuff but undeniably true. Paul and I talk, we meet people and talk to them. Then we stop for lunch in a shady place full of lush grass where we can take off the saddles and check for sores. All are in good condition so we breathe a sigh of relief, relax and look for the lunch we meant to pack for ourselves, but have left on the kitchen table at home. Typical! We stop and buy a cake from a Patisserie later along the way – all good practice.

Of course nothing ever goes entirely to plan and if it did I would worry that I was missing something. Some 10 kilometres from our destination the path becomes impassable for a number of reasons: a fallen tree that we might have been able to negotiate if we had removed all the saddles, but just beyond this is an electric fence and a field of cows. Someone doesn't want us to go on, so we have no alternative but to turn round and take the main road into St. Mars sur la Futaie where we will plan to stay.

Riding on any kind of busy road is a dangerous business, however safe the horse. Some drivers slow down, but most do not and our horses are still unaccustomed to vehicles passing at great speed, particularly large lorries. Plus, we have a little dog whose road sense is still developing. We decide that he will have to ride in front of Paul's saddle because my hands are already full with leading Okapi, but I am concerned because it is a lot to ask of a rider with less than three months' experience. What happens if Vasco starts to slip or Lubie takes fright and Paul needs both hands on the reins? Then I have my own brief moment of pure genius (a rare occurrence) and find the solution. We can clip his harness to a hook on Paul's belt. That way Vasco can sit securely on the saddle roll without any danger of slipping and without needing to be held. It works and we find a temporary solution that we will develop later to ensure that the clip is easy to attach whenever necessary. The horses perform well too. I take the lead, and in spite of some minor swerves and hysteria on Gwen's part, we are able to pick up the track again a few kilometres further on, though we have added another 8 to our total distance.

On reaching the very pleasant *Auberge* we find that we have it all to ourselves. The horses are given a small field for the night and access to feed that we had not expected, meaning we are able to reward them with double the amount we had brought ourselves. After saying goodnight, we treat ourselves to a shower and a huge meal. Meanwhile, Vasco is happy to be left in the room where he sleeps without a murmur until the morning. 35 kilometres is a long way for any dog and particularly one with legs that are shorter than the length of my forearm, but he has clearly loved every minute of the journey.

Over dinner we chat comfortably with Sabina, the young German girl who is looking after us. She is an artist by profession and her French husband is a jazz musician, but they are having to work in the hotel until they get the breaks they need. Paul mentions that I play the saxophone, and I qualify this by saying that I do so very badly, but it is an opening to a very welcome invitation to a jazz evening the following week. Surprising where rides with horses can take you.

After that we have to get down to taking stock of our first taste of long distance riding. We have not pushed ourselves or our horses, but we have gone further than we intended and still feel surprisingly fit. The horses have shown absolutely no signs of tiring and even though Okapi was beginning to slow down it was more a matter of asking the proverbial *Are we nearly there yet*? question, rather than any serious problems on his part. On the human side, Paul's back has not even twinged and though my backside is sore I know it will harden up.

High spots have been many and varied, but perhaps the most notable was meeting the man with his Haflinger stallion in a cart with a foal tethered alongside. After the initial introductory questions he tells us that he also intends to do a small section of the [5]*Chemin de St. Jacques* during his August vacation, and will drop by our house with some information about places to stay with horses. Better still, we have had no great problems to speak of, at least nothing that got the better of us. The only negative point was when we noticed that Gwen had lost a boot. An expensive lesson that tells us that we must be more vigilant, check each other's horse at regular intervals and carry spares.

The next day, our return is equally pleasant and with only a few minor incidents that can only increase our ability to cope. In one place a succession of farms seems to possess every dog of every breed and every size, culminating in a pair of St. Bernards. Vasco does his best to stand up to them all and protect his team, even chasing off a particularly vicious pair, but a large black dog that leaps out unexpectedly from a very suburban type of house is just too much. It bites Gwen and sends her rocketing, ballistic style, into Lubie's rump. I shout 'hang on' to Paul, but he is already clinging limpet-style, so we all survive. Gwen is physically unharmed, though her mental scars run deep, as she keeps reminding me every time a dog barks in the distance. Later on, we encounter a narrow opening between two poles designed to deter anyone who is anything more than skeletal. Horses, bikes and transport of that ilk are definitely not wanted. Once again we face failure and an impossibly long detour, so we opt for a limited form of vandalism, by lifting one pole out (with difficulty) and putting it back (with care) once we have passed through.

So what have learnt from our first trip?

Take care of our boots, keep an eye out for each other's horse and add spares to our kit.

The collapsible bucket (currently travelling between France and Canada with the pack saddle) will be vital for getting water to the horses when cattle troughs are on the other side of fences we can't get through.

Vasco will run until he drops, but we must watch out for his pads and general fitness.

The multipurpose foam pad we had bought for flexible interchange between our bums and the horses' backs is too easy to flip off and forget, which I did.

Talcum powder must be added the list of things to pack, for reasons I will let the readers imagine. Likewise, I must go out and buy some sensible knickers.

Okapi must be taught to appreciate that as a pack horse he is a great deal wider than before. Some work is needed from us on this, because we narrowly avoided an accident when he caught one rucksack on a bridge and broke a strap.

This is going to be the trip of a lifetime though, if all goes well, not the last.

PAUL - ON VERTIGO

The thing about vertigo is that it is rarely rational. Whenever I take one of those open ski lifts that clatter over the dizzily high pylons, I tell myself that thousands have done this safely before me, but the sweat on my brow, damp hands and frozen stare betray the panic that is going on inside. I am convinced that gravity has singled me out to suck my leaden skis and rigid body down to a messy death. How on earth do all those other people manage to look so happy? How have they become inured to the experience? If I manage to hang on long enough could I be just as blasé too? Perhaps this is why I am on a horse trying to pretend to the world and myself that I am normal, or just that little bit more than normal.

The good news is that two weeks before we set off my wrist is fully recovered after the fall from Okapi and I am managing, mainly, to dispel the sense that any unexpected twitch beneath the saddle could result in another nose dive into the asphalt. Lubie is proving to be very special. In horse speak she is "bomb proof". She ignores barking dogs, noisy tractors towing an array of hay making equipment, juggernauts that pass too close and even the braying of a randy stallion. Plus, she is good on her feet, staying upright on rocks, shingle and mud where Gwen will have been sliding on her backside long before.

So now all I need to do is accept that Lubie knows better and trust her judgement. But then again there is the green plastic sheeting, the stuff used by fastidious French gardeners to suppress weeds. It's everywhere and relatively innocuous to the likes of you and me, but for Lubie the mere sight of it is reason enough to perform a 180 degree turn in a single stride. When something like this happens experience really counts. There is just no thinking time. Lean back (of course the body always wants to go forward). Clench knees (though as Babette tells me, they are meant to be in contact all the time). Shorten reins (I can do that bit because they're the only thing I've got to grab on to). Anyway, in spite of myself I survive and through this learn that Lubie's particular cocktail of fears (which is hopefully less exotic than my own) has a green plastic base.

On the practical side, it seems that our preparations are at last falling into place. We have acquired a full set of guide books for the French (*le sentier Grand Randonnée* – GR65) and Spanish sections of the *Chemin*. These are the Topo-guides from the *Federation Francaise de la Randonnée Pédestre*, which though excellent, are designed primarily for walkers and lack anything more than the most basic information for riders. However, with these and a little web work I am slowly building up a directory of the places where we can lodge or buy hard food for the horses. The websites of the *Committee Nationale de Tourisme Equestre* and the *Federation Francaise d'Equestre* have been invaluable.

Our recent weekend away has told us that at our present level of fitness we can handle thirty-five kilometres per day in the terrain and temperatures of Northern France. However, I know we cannot count on this in the South and that problems and challenges will be the order of the day. As a result, and probably because of my desire not to readopt the shackles of the project management methods we both laboured under when employed, my focus is now on ensuring that we have enough information to enable us to make good decisions hour by hour, rather than relying on a fixed schedule.

One of our major concerns has been the transport of the horses down to Le Puy en Velay, 750 kilometres from home. But our ever widening circle of helpful and enthusiastic friends has turned up a second trailer so now we can tick this item off the list. We have also secured a booking at an Equine Centre at St. Paulien, just 14 kilometres away from Le Puy en Velay, where we plan to stay for two nights to allow horses and humans to recover from the long journey south.

Then, just one hour ago in fact, the final, vital piece of missing equipment was delivered, our Canadian pack saddle, complete with two cavernous bags that will easily accommodate camping gear, horse food, tools and computer kit. Only the rain, which is thundering down now as I write, has saved Okapi from a fitting session and subsequent catwalk display to show off his new outfit. But with any luck the weather will improve tomorrow, though on this point Okapi may not be entirely in agreement.

With these final items crossed off, we now move one step nearer to the cliff edge and prepare to invite the whole commune to watch us jump off. Vertigo and insanity seem to go hand in hand, but I'm mad enough not to care.

No Turning Back

'Only six days to go. You must be getting really excited.' Cat says, and yes I suppose I should be, but actually I'm feeling quite low for a variety of poorly defined reasons.

The farewell barbecue is worrying, though less so than previously, because friends have rallied round to help, but I have acquired other worries to fill the gap. First, there is the pile of kit on our sofa which seems to grow by the day. The cavernous pack bags will accommodate it, but Okapi may not be able to manage the weight. Then there is the folly, pure and simple, of what we are doing when we could be gardening at home with far less expense and risk. But these are questions I can deal with, so what is this really about? Come on, deep breath and time for honesty …. It's about Lucy, my sixteen-year-old daughter.

'We've always done everything together, just you and me, but it's all so different now,' she complained a few days ago while Paul and I were busily planning routes, and of course she is right, though it is not Paul who has changed the balance.

Growing up is so very hard to do. The phrase rattles round my head as I write. It comes from a song or something, though at the moment I can't recall the exact source. Growing up/growing old, it's all the same anyway; difficult and painful.

Lucy must grow away from us and establish her independence in an environment where it is still safe to make mistakes. She has achieved the impossible for an English child, coming third in her year after effectively three years in a French school (the trauma of transition from England to France rendering the first year entirely useless). Now she just has the Brevet to deal with before launching herself into the almost adult world of boarding at the *Lycée* in September. It's a tall order and she must use this summer without our protection to develop her confidence and ability to exist independently. She has a lot of good friends, but some are obsessed with boys and can't understand that she has other priorities – the usual teenage pressures - but alone they can be hard to deal with, so travelling with us would be the easier option.

I am nervous for all of us. I will miss her and wish that she could see what we are seeing and learn what we are learning. Every day I will wonder if I have done the right thing, but if anything goes wrong she won't phone because she'll want to show her independence and I won't want to push. Meanwhile Paul, who is always practical and caring in these situations does his best to understand, but will only be able to gauge our moods by the way we take them out on him. Poor man.

On the positive side, Okapi has taken to his new pack saddle, we have all the equipment we think we need, the horses are fit and sleek and the daily salt ration is being eaten without complaint. So, in reality I don't have a lot to complain about. We are more or less on schedule and the only item left uncrossed on our list is the Equine dentist's visit, because he seems to have disappeared off the face of the earth. Though even here the news is good in that both Gwen and Lubie have stopped spitting. Perhaps it was just a passing phase, much like the grey cloud I've been under. And guess what? Just a few days later, while I am still preoccupied with being moody and miserable, the dreaded village barbecue comes and goes without incident. In fact, it is pronounced a resounding success. How did that happen?

From what I can remember, about sixty people turned up, many of whom we knew reasonably well, but equally many who we recognised only as a head in a passing car or tractor. Our poor French floundered, but the conversation went on regardless and we were touchingly asked to autograph the cockles shells we had served up with filling as the starter. Then, with the food finished, though not the drinking, our horses contributed to the highlight of the day, led by a small boy called Harry.

Harry is the eight-year-old son of friends who live close by. He has cerebral palsy and is unable to walk, but on Lucy's old pony (and more recently Lubie) he is as mobile as the rest of us. So Harry and Lubie strutted their stuff and everyone applauded, but one person in particular was more than just impressed.

Gerard is the mayor's assistant in the little village of St Aubin Fosse Louvain where we live. He is forty and also has cerebral palsy. Who knows what went through Gerard's head as he watched Harry riding, but shortly after he announced that he wanted to do the same, dismissing his mother when she tried to dissuade him, and asking only that someone bring him a chair to stand on. Paul, Christien and another of our friends, Dave, rushed to assist, while I held Lubie and did my best to calm her. I had no idea of how she would react to the sensation of his severe tremors on her back.

True to form our equine angel stood and waited, only her flickering ears indicating that she was in the least concerned. And then we walked, slowly at first and gradually in ever increasing circles as Gerard's expression relaxed into a broad grin. It was only when we stopped after ten minutes or so that I realised everyone was watching us in complete silence and Christien, our macho farmer friend, was crying.

FRENCH SECTION

LE PUY EN VELAY

TO

THE PYRENEES

An adventure must always begin. Mine began with a picture book. I was ten.
From These Are My People, by Alan Marshall

After all the time and trauma we only have a few things left to sort out. One of the main priorities is the second trailer we have been leant by Didier, a local farmer. Fine for cattle, but not a cosseted pony due to travel for ten hours. I look at what needs to be done and sigh, it's too wide, he'll fall and hurt himself if we don't pad it out with straw bales and line the slippery floor with an old carpet, but this is nothing when compared to the main problem – no ramp. Unlike cattle, horses are not prepared to leap a metre up into the unknown. I don't know what to do, but push the problem to the back of my mind and tell myself something will come up.

The good news is that the pack bags I had sworn would be too heavy, are actually under the maximum permissible weight for a young pony of Okapi's size. We have scrimped and scraped and thrown out everything except the most vital equipment, and now the scales tell us that we can put stuff back in. I begin to feel better, until Paul announces that we have to be up at five in the morning, though I only have myself to blame for this, because I have insisted that we must do everything we can to avoid the heat whilst travelling.

Cat and Ray (my ex-husband), who are doing the driving for us, arrive on time and are distressingly chirpy. Everyone else is on time too, including Lubie and Gwen who have been trying to get into the trailer all night, because they have smelt the hay. The packs go in the back of Cat's car, saddles and the rest go in our jeep, we hitch the second trailer and now there's nothing left to do except load Okapi. I look at Cat and she looks at me. We are supposed to be the experienced ones. Lucy says nothing, but I can feel her eyes boring through the back of my head. This is one person I cannot fool.

'Let him take a good look first.' I say authoritatively. 'He's willing enough when he knows what we're asking of him.' I'm not half as confident as I sound, but Okapi makes up the short fall by taking one look at the hay inside and stepping calmly aboard without a backward glance. I try not to look too amazed.

Ten hours later, with stops in between to offer water and replenish hay, we arrive at our destination in St. Paulien – a charming livery yard and riding stable where the welcoming family have already prepared a paddock for our horses. It's perfect. They unload calmly and launch themselves at their food as if we had just driven five miles from home. This bodes well, the only negative point being when the owner recognises Gwen as a traditional French Trotter, informing me that they are famous for falling over their own noses and crossing their feet. It explains a lot about the problems I have experienced with her, but does nothing for my confidence.

We have chosen to start from Le Puy en Velay, smack bang in the middle of the Massif Central and a range of extinct volcanoes (Le Puy means volcano), because this route seems to offer the most interesting and possibly challenging ride in terms of the terrain, but the town is entirely theatrical and bizarre.

As we approach, the first thing we see is a great looming six-metre-high statue of the Virgin and Child glowering down from its pinnacle of rock known as Rocher Corneille. Perhaps even more bizarrely still, the statue has been cast from 213 guns captured in Sebastopol and coloured to match the tiled roofs below. As I gaze upwards, shivers run down my spine and I wonder if I am the only one to see the irony.

In the afternoon Lucy, Paul and I visit the cathedral, Notre-Dame du Puy, and again it is obvious that the designers have gone for maximum impact. We stand under the five-storied western front like a trio of garden gnomes staring into an apple tree. It's so vast that it can only be photographed from the other side of town, and I nearly break my neck trying to walk down a flight of stairs backwards. Ostensibly, our reason for being here is to follow the pilgrim ritual and purge ourselves of sin so that we start out with clean slate, though in reality this can only ever be a token exercise for us - we are neither religious nor Roman Catholic. But it doesn't matter, because in our view a moment's reflection in a quiet place can achieve just as much, so we enter the cathedral and let the atmosphere to do the rest, a rare moment of mutual silence, during which we find ourselves drifting apart in the shadows to find a place alone. No doubt this can be attributed to our general frame of mind and susceptibility, but we are all struck by the sensation of walking into an operational place of worship, as opposed to the often sterile and empty ambience of churches only visited by tourists like ourselves. We later agree that we want to attend mass and find ourselves once again profoundly moved as a result, though none of us can explain exactly why. On the more practical side, we also take time out to get our pilgrim passports stamped, with Lucy being an honorary attendant on the basis that she will be joining us at some point later on the way.

Not Switzerland, less terrible. Not Italy, less beautiful. George Sand.

Day One of our epic journey and Paul stops the jeep and trailer opposite a small dirt track, pronouncing solemnly that this is the St. James Way (or because we are in France, *Le Chemin de St. Jacques*). I had expected something more distinguished, a few cobbles at the very least. For ease we have chosen to mount the horses and warm them up just outside St. Polignac in the Velay, 10 kilometres before Le Puy. We are standing on a volcanic plateau of outstanding beauty, or so I'm told, but I'm incapable of appreciating the landscape. For a start it's freezing and my birthday present jacket is meant for summer temperatures, plus the wind is blowing a hefty gale which makes the horses skitty and impatient while being tacked up. This is when I realise that we have never actually put all the pack bags on before. Paul and Lucy ask me what's this bit and where does that go, but I don't know and even if I did I wouldn't be able to see anything because I'm ctying my eyes out. Why am I leaving my daughter? What on earth possessed me to argue that it was the sensible thing to do? And Paul is no better. He's blubbering too. What a bloody mess, but after all the time we have put into this the only choice we have is to put up and shut up. Then we turn and wave to Ray and my saddle roll slips off.

'Paul are you sure about this? I mean we could call this a test run and just ... why are you laughing?'

Actually, from here it goes surprisingly well. The track is easy to follow and the horses are keen to go. On reaching Le Puy en Velay, we negotiate heavy traffic and bemused drivers without too much difficulty, apart from Okapi's no-warning, arm-wrenching poo stops. Then we arrive in front of the cathedral, at the bottom of the steps where, in 950, the first non-Spanish pilgrim, Godescalc Bishop of Le Puy, embarked on his pilgrimage too. For complete authenticity I suppose we should have climbed them and started from the main door in the west front, but I decide that in view of Gwen's various genetic difficulties, we should just take the well sign-posted St. James Way, which passes through at their base. Just one problem: it's lunch time and the narrow alley is full of tables – well, it is called La Rue des Tables.

I don't trust any of our horses to negotiate this lot without sideswiping a family and their lunch, so we have no alternative but to find another route via the small back streets and would you believe it – unavoidable steps. What now? I feel queasy, but when Paul asks me if we can do it, I lie and nod because there is no other option. Here goes. Gwen snorts, defies gravity, French Trotter's disease and all her other myriad disadvantages, and ten minutes later we are on level ground, grappling with the indisputable fact that it was our ugly duckling who got us here.

Our euphoria does not last long. On the other side of Le Puy en Velay we are reminded that the route is taking us through a range of volcanoes that must have had a particularly bad case of wind when they off loaded their magma. Suddenly the flat and favourable terrain has turned into a big dipper. Within the first few metres the pack saddle starts to slip sideways, backwards and forwards, all at the same time. My spirits plummet. Why didn't I invest more time in learning how to pack it? I had told myself and Paul that I would, but then so many other things were happening at the time. Excuses! Excuses! All irrelevant, as we are forced to struggle on, dismounting at frequent intervals to set the pack bags straight again. Then one of Gwen's saddle bags splits, ripping literally down a complete side, proving that buying cheap does not always work, but regrets won't mend anything so we patch it as best we can and move on until we eventually reach Montbonnet, a hill top village that seems to move further away with each weary step.

By the time we arrive, we are all knackered: horses, humans and dog, but we have to unload and stow our gear in a shed, while the proprietor of the *gîte d'etape* hovers over us nervously because we are taking so long. His wife serves dinner at 7.00 and not a minute later he tells us, so we do our best to be punctual, though in hindsight it would have been better to be late.

The first and second courses are passable, but the cheese comes with the added extra of maggots, as I find out two mouthfuls in. My appetite evaporates and I retire to bed with the beginnings of a migraine that I hope will work itself out while I sleep. I want to go home. I am worried about the horses – we have put them in a field close to a main road with only a swamp at one end for water. I am having to hide Vasco in the bunk, because at the last minute Madame informs me that he must stay downstairs (you must be joking). Worse still, I am also discovering that *gîte d'etape* means sharing dormitories with anyone who pitches up, in our case a Belgian with steaming underpants and a snore that must have been heard the length of the St. James Way. I sleep intermittently, my head still pounding.

Morning light and I feel sick. The migraine is still with me and we have to get our kit together and go. Paul is endlessly patient and sympathetic and does the major share of work, though he's probably cursing me under his breath. The good news is that the horses have coped well and throw themselves at their breakfast with enthusiasm. Our spirits rise with the sun and as the countryside opens out into broad expanses of volcanic architecture, the joy of riding is easier to recall. Blue and yellow butterflies lift in clouds around us and when my beloved Gwen negotiates a particularly difficult rocky outcrop without complaint or accident, I realise that my migraine has gone too.

CONGENITALLY CLUMSY FRENCH TROTTER

The next day has no moments of light relief, but my own ignorance is primarily to blame. Dense contour lines on a map mean very little to me, so when Paul points them out while we are mooching along a gently undulating track, I decide that he is being simply being over-dramatic. Then we hit the first descent. A perpendicular rock face that I wouldn't even want to tackle in climbing boots. Worse still, we can't turn back, because the path is too narrow and the only way is down.

I pretend to know what I am doing and take the lead, but within seconds Gwen has lost control of her feet and her bowels and I'm not much better off. Meanwhile, Lubie scrambles down behind Paul mountain goat style, revealing yet another aspect of her already perfect disposition. Okapi copes as one would expect from a pony; nimble and unperturbed, until the pack saddle slides up over his ears.

Who said the pack was light? Paul and I have to lift the bags on and off at least twenty times, carrying them down the greater part of the descent ourselves, while the horses are tethered at various points on the treacherously steep path. This is where we find that for Lubie a dropped rein means freedom. She is not sure where she is going, but it doesn't stop her heading off at a trot on a perpendicular rock face, meaning that we have to chase after her at top speed when we are barely capable of crawling. Gwen, adds to my personal pain by whinnying piteously every time I have to leave her, then a pilgrim caps it all by asking whether we really thought we should be here. Have you got any better ideas?

At the bottom, drenched in sweat and totally exhausted, we manage a group hug with some incredulity. We are still alive. If the horses had been wearing iron shoes, which slip on any kind of smooth surface, the outcome would have been unthinkably different. Then it occurs to me that the difficulties we have had with the pack saddle are entirely my fault. I should have included a [6]breast plate and [7]crupper in the kit. These would have prevented it from sliding either forwards or backwards, and as the person who is supposed to know about this horsy stuff I should have thought about them. I admit my oversight to Paul, but he typically refuses to lay any blame. Later we read in the guidebook that the route we have negotiated is unsuitable for bikes, it says nothing about horses.

In Monistrol d'Allier every bed is filled by a Japanese party, though strangely enough we haven't seen them on the way here, but after last night I don't care, because this means we have to go one step upmarket and pay a little more for a bed in a *chambre d'hôte*. In fact, the service is better than you'd get in the Ritz (or as I imagine you'd get). Madame et Monsieur welcome us warmly, offer to do our washing and give Vasco his very own mat to sleep on in our room. I haven't the heart to tell them that the dog is ridiculously spoilt and will only sleep on our bed. The horses are slightly less comfortably accommodated, because every square metre of the village has been built on a gradient of 1 in 5, the field is head high in unidentifiable weeds and there is no water. We spend most of the evening slogging up and down the 300 metre distance, between the graveyard where there is a tap, and their field.

In spite of all this, we find them alive and well in the morning, though they have broken through the fence that should have separated them from a row of expensive looking solar panels. Fortunately, there is no damage and we patch the fence up as best we can, but while we are tacking up, Lubie marches through it again and reveals yet another aspect of her multi-faceted personality - she is the equine version of Houdini, with about as much determination.

The next day's ride to Chanaleilles is tough, but not nearly so tough. We encounter some stiff climbs where Gwen finds her own very special strength, endurance. While Lubie struggles and loses her usual sprinting enthusiasm. Okapi is good too, though he still hasn't got used to his new pack pony width. Anyone following behind could track us down by the bent signposts and inverted wing mirrors he leaves in his wake. But we are all learning and better still, necessity being the mother of all invention (or some such cliché), the need for a breastplate and a crupper has exercised our minds sufficiently for us to come up with a reasonable solution. We are using an elastic [8]surcingle to wrap around either the front or back of Okapi, depending on whether we are going up or down, and it seems to work. Riding is becoming easier and we manage a steep 400 metre climb without stopping once. Hey! This is fun!

While walking we are surprised by the progress of a middle aged couple in front of us – they walk at more or less the same speed as we do and don't seem to slow even when a mountain suddenly erupts in front of them. This makes me wonder about the wisdom of using horses at all. It takes longer for us to prepare in the morning and we have more equipment and more worry, but as Paul keeps reminding me, this is not a race. We also discover the truth of that other cliché - you can lead a horse to water but you can't make it drink. Our horses are convinced that the water troughs (found in just about every village we pass through) have teeth and claws hidden at their base. Lubie, the only one of our team with any sense at all, drinks a little, but Gwen and Okapi continue to snort and cavort until we are forced to get the collapsible bucket out and give them water by hand. Rivers receive much the same response and I worry about the inevitable moment when we will have to cross one.

Meanwhile the countryside has opened out into a rolling sequence of hillsides, remote villages and forests. I can sense by our mutual silence that the infinite expanses are filling our minds in a way that the more comfortable paths between towns had not. Before long we are dropping into the pilgrim vernacular and managing to wish the people we meet a *bonne route*. We also discover sufficient French vocabulary for answering questions about where we started from, how far we are going, how many kilometres we do a day and where we are staying tonight. In between, we have to smile modestly when people congratulate us on intending to 'go all the way', and send a non-verbal piss-off to those who stare back disbelievingly. It's going to take me a few more weeks before I will accept their slightly scathing comments about horses only doing the same speed and distance as people, but Paul manages to deliver, without wincing, the holier-than-thou response that we are here to appreciate the journey. But French is not the only language we have to stutter through. Within the space of a few days we have met a vast number of nationalities: Swiss, Belgian, Italian, Spanish and German, and are even beginning to recognise some familiar faces.

Our *gîte* for the night is in a village off the main route and we have it entirely to ourselves, which makes a pleasant change. The only worrying aspect is that the horses are to be accommodated in the garden of the house itself, which has a steep sided stream running through it, further complicated by a narrow concrete bridge. As I watch Lubie roll and nearly fall in, I am all too aware that we are taking our horses to places where no sensible horse person would go, but I suppose this is all part of the experience and I will die before I let any harm come to them. We put the bells on Lubie and Okapi, because the entrance is only closed over with a piece of white tape and our washing. Later, the girls stare into our bedroom with disbelief written all over the faces. I suspect they've never seen a naked human before and they're obviously not impressed.

At four in the morning we are woken by rolling thunder, streaks of lightening and a cacophony of bells. There is a storm overhead, the tack is outside and the horses are cantering round the garden. We race out and do our best to retrieve the gear and calm the equines. It's fortunate that the house is at the edge of the village with no overlooking neighbours, because we are once again butt-naked.

HEALTH AND PERFORMANCE REVIEW:

Paul's bum is in need of treatment with talc and creme.

My rear is less troubled, because I have been using a saddle cushion, but my shoulders are feeling the strain of the jolt from Okapi's lead rein when he stops suddenly.

Vasco is suffering from the heat and the distance, but riding with Paul more now and coping better as a result.

Gwen is showing signs of a rubbed heel, perhaps a small piece of the very sharp volcanic rock has got into her boot.

Today we are heading for Aumont-Aubrac, a small town in a valley of the Aubrac mountain range, squeezed into a wedge of windswept uplands lying to the east of the River Truyere and north of the
Lot valley. The highest points are between 1200 and 1400

metres and today we will reach 1290. Without the steady stream of pilgrims there would be more cows than people here, well in fact there probably are anyway. If the sun was not shining I would describe this this place bleak and miserable, but today it is just plain spectacular. A wilderness, where it is easy to imagine that the legendary *Bete du Gevaudan*, a ferocious, man-eating wolf, could still exist, though I can't help wondering how people manage to survive in the unbelievably remote farms and exquisite villages built out of the stubby granite rock. Meanwhile, our horses create a lot of interest with the locals, and hysteria on the part of a group of American women.

'Can I stroke your horse?'

'Do they bite?'

'Aren't they just the most beautiful thing you've ever seen?

Gwen plays her part and avoids treading on anybody, so I presume that in spite of her previous behaviour, she must enjoy human company.

As we enter the edges of civilisation again, we find that the route planners have only taken pedestrians into account. In St. Alban sur Limangole we are sent the wrong way up one-way streets and though the horses perform well, we do not manage to buy food so that we can perhaps camp [9]*au sauvage* later (total intake today two granola bars). We also meet the Belgian again – having lunch in a pavement café. How does he manage to be ahead of us when he sleeps late and we have seen nothing of him on the route?

Babette Gallard

Houdini

After this we slog on until we reach Aumont-Aubrac and find a *gîte d'etape* attached to the local hotel. The owners take horses, but we have to rig up a temporary fence on a large piece of grass. Just like the good Boy Scout, Paul is always prepared and he has packed the white tape horses usually associate with an electric fence, so ten minutes later the horses are inside and we can see to ourselves.

We have a good meal, too much wine and fall into bed, only to be woken half an hour later by the waiter who had served us drinks in the bar. The horses are loose. We hurtle out, still barely awake and barely dressed, but actually it's not as bad as we had feared. Lubie and Gwen have been caught by another member of staff and Okapi is snuffling around nearby. They just wanted the greener grass on the other side, and now understanding that Lubie is the culprit in any misdemeanour of this kind we tether her firmly to a tree, put the others back into their enclosure and sleep relatively soundly for the rest of the night. Only relatively, because my head is spinning with the thoughts of the already narrowly missed disasters and those that are still to come. Why take these risks? Why don't we turn back now while we can and before something really terrible happens? Then the sun pours in through the window above me and of course it is already too late to change my mind.

HEALTH AND PERFORMANCE REVIEW:

Gwen is still convinced that manholes, stones and water are the most dangerous phenomena on this earth. Today we had to walk over a stone bridge no wider than her hooves, because neither she, nor any of the others, will go through water. At least they are now drinking from troughs.

Equipment is working well, but already suffering from wear and tear.

Vasco is doing much better in the cooler temperature.

Poo-stops are becoming a problem. Any horsy person reading this will insist that horses should not be allowed to stop, but I say that consideration has to be given when the rides are anything up to ten hours a day. Nevertheless, Gwen's habit of stopping just when Okapi is closest so that her poo falls directly either on to or into our pack bags is unpleasant, particularly when it involves our food.

Gwen's near hind heel showing worrying signs of sponginess with some discharge. We need to watch this carefully.

Lucy has passed her Brevet!!

The next day's riding across the mountains of Aubrac is even more spectacular, and though the wind is blowing an exfoliating gale, nothing can dull the euphoria. Then, suddenly, the mountain tops flatten out into a plateau covered with vast granite boulders. The word huge simply does not do them justice, but I can't find any other. Everything is bigger than anything I have seen or imagined before. Paul tries to quantify the kind of volcanic force required to hurl colossi of this magnitude, while I prefer to simply imagine what the landscape would have looked like in its more explosive era. We each have our own way of appreciating the moment.

Half way into our day we start to see hoof prints that look very recent, and shortly after meet up with a French-woman leading a small pony with her young daughter on its back. She tells us that she, and her other children who are ahead, do a section of the *Chemin* every year and hope to finish it entirely within four more years. This will surely become a major component of the family memory, with each member having his or her own specialist view according to the age and outlook at the time. I think of Lucy again. What on earth made me believe that it would be better for her to stay at home?

In the same village where we have stopped to chat, we also meet a woman who has done the entire *Chemin du Puy* on horseback. She is very enthusiastic about our plans and shows us a picture of her own horse. The boots interest her too and she is keen to know more, so we tell her about our experience. Less positively, she concludes by saying that she'd decided not to do the Spanish section because it was supposed to be very difficult due to problems with taking horses into Spain for any length of time, accommodation and the like. Paul and I exchange worried glances, but we can only meet the challenges as they come and hope that things have either improved or she is wrong.

From here we scrap our plans to have a short day, because everything seems to being going so well and there are no regrets on this. We find an equestrian centre where the horses are given a decent field and some dry food. A good reward for good work. We are also able to get a night's sleep without worrying about what they are up to – the first since we started out.

Babette Gallard

WHO FORGOT TO TELL FRANCE IT WAS SUMMER?

Passing squalls of rain stung shadowed patches of water into an agitated leaping. The spiked reeds quivered and bent to wet gusts, gusts that drove upon our faces and made the horses tuck their heads low on their chests.
From These Are My People, by Alan Marshall

Riding the Milky Way

Our target for today is to reach Saint-Chély-d'Aubrac but it's not much fun in the pouring rain. We climb up to 1368 metres and traverse the bleakest moors imaginable, where past pilgrims used to be able to count on 'the bell of the lost' from Notre Dame des Pauvres for guidance. We don't hear it and miss the path for a while. The only positive aspect of this being that the horses temporarily conquer their fear of water, because trying to avoid the stuff becomes a useless exercise.

Five minutes after starting out Lubie inexplicably casts a boot and a girl walking close behind helpfully offers to pick it up, and so we meet Bettina, a young German in her gap year that only fate in a good mood could have put our way. Bettina and I chat and discover a mutual interest and experience of working with horses in Germany, which makes slogging through the pouring rain marginally less unpleasant. She opens the many gates that cross our path and saves us the hassle of dismounting.

On arrival in Saint-Chély-d'Aubrac, not much more than a line of houses focussed around the pilgrim trade, the rain is still pouring down and our already low spirits are not helped by the fact that the first *gîte* we find has no obvious signs of a place to keep horses. We walk down to the only other *gîte* in the vicinity, where the owner informs us that the *Mairie* has a place to put horses, so we trudge back up a distressingly steep hill, to find that the *Mairie* is, of course, closed (life in France has taught us that the *Mairie* is never open when you need it to be). as we linger disconsolately near the door someone stops his car to say that the field is on the other side of the river.

Sometime later, after much, wearisome stopping of passers-by to ask where the field actually is, we find it across a very pretty little bridge and my heart skips a beat. Horse-heaven, shady and full of rich, belly high grass, but of course there is a problem – it is a long way from the *gîte* and there is nowhere to leave our saddles. Then I see a man bent over what appear to be small piles of bark. We take a closer look and find that this is an escargot farm. I didn't even know such places existed, but from what I can gather this one is a very respectable free range version. We exchange pleasantries and he says that he has no objection to our using some of his space to pitch our tent, so as per the advert, Paul chucks it in the air and within a total of ten seconds we are able to throw our equipment inside.

Meanwhile Bettina has gone ahead to reserve our beds in the *gîte* and the rain has stopped. Life is looking up and as we leave, Gwen bellows as if to say that she feels the same too. Inside, when we pull out our sleeping bags and check our gear, the news is not so good. Everything is soaking and we can only look forward to a humid night. Still, a hot shower followed by wine can induce temporary amnesia, so we take the former and then find a restaurant next door for the latter.

The Belgian arrives in time for the cheese, dishevelled like most walkers that day, but also clearly drunk. We greet him with hypocritical smiles and then shrink back into our corner to bathe in London's glory – London will host the next Olympics, but this is not the place to cheer too loudly.

Later that night, the top bunk of the bed I am sharing with Paul shakes as if a volcano has erupted and then the underpants appear. The Belgian is back.

…AND HE RESTED ON THE SEVENTH DAY (GEN. 2:2-3)

This morning is our last in the Auvergne and we are coming out of the Aubrac Mountains to drop down into the Lot Region. I can't say I am sorry. Our target is Espalion over twenty k's away and we get up respectably early and find a note in our still damp boots. Our friends, Nick, Karen and their three children, Danielle, George and Harry, have found us and are camping down the road. Then, just as we are about to leave, Danielle opens the door and tells us that they have tracked us all the way down the St. James Way, asking people if they had seen two people, three horses and a dog. Clearly we have been noticed. We arrange to meet them in Espalion where they had already planned to camp. Then we go down to the horses and find that the little black pony has joined them. The woman tells us that she and her poor family had been lost on the moors for nearly two hours the day before.

The weather is still unsympathetic, with an iron sky and biting wind that slices through us on the long exposed descents. Bettina has gone on ahead and we are back to tackling any difficulties on our own. We encounter a fallen tree that even dismounted is too low to go under, and an old bridge that is a tightrope walk for the horses. Nevertheless, we manage both and I convince myself that on foot all of this would appear charming and picturesque. Soon after, we ride into the medieval village of Saint Côme-d'Olt with its twisted church spire. I have never seen anything like this before, though Paul tells me that Chesterfield in England has one too. The route takes us through winding streets and alleys, cobbled and lined with houses that are almost too perfect in their quaint antiquity. Paul wonders why their geraniums seem so much healthier and densely coloured than ours and I suggest the obvious in terms of the climate, while noticing that my own skin colour has become deep and richly golden since our departure. Then we cross the Lot and from there enjoy a gentle and pleasant ride along the Lot Valley, which makes me think of Joanne Harris's book Five Quarters of an Orange (even though it is set on the Loire). Looking at the emerald shadows, I can easily imagine the ancient pike lurking there and, because I am a keen swimmer, the challenge of crossing the currents is almost irresistible, though the temperature of the water isn't.

From the outset, we had planned to rest every seven days and a rest day is just what we need now. Gwen's rubbed heel is not looking good. We have picked a good place too. Espalion is in the middle of the fertile Lot Valley and would have been the first sniff of humanity and food the pilgrims got after staggering down from the Aubrac plateau. I know just how they must have felt and launch myself into the excesses of tourism without the slightest feeling of guilt; made all the easier because it's market day. Paul and I read about the museums we should visit and the people we should know (composer - Francis Poulenc, inventor of diving suits - Louis Denayrouze), but stick our noses into a hundred varieties of cheese and stuff ourselves with cakes and coffee instead. When we get back to our books in the evening, I learn about Guibert, an unfortunate pilgrim who was attacked by a band of robbers and had his eyes ripped out and taken by birds to Conques. Ultimately, he was able to continue after his sight had been finally restored via Sainte Foy and the fervour of worshipping pilgrims. All of which makes me wonder if our, less spiritual but no less energetic fervour, could do anything like this for Gwen?

The war, that in cities brooded over streets, became remote and unreal. In the cities, the blackout was menacing and unnatural. It concealed a dread and pressed on one like a burden, but here the dark nights were unconcerned and still.

From These Are My People, by Alan Marshall

Overshadowing all this selfish and comfortable activity is the news that a series of bombs went off in

London yesterday. The parallel with Alan Marshall's own experience fifty years ago is all too obvious. Nothing has changed in the intervening time. Individuals are still being caught up in the maelstrom of ambitions and doctrines that have so little to do with their daily lives. Paul and I did not want the war, do not support the exploitation of Iraq in the name of freedom, would never wish the cruelties perpetrated by either side, but have only avoided death or injury ourselves because we are lucky enough to be here and not there. We spend the rest of the day in moral debate and are probably fairly miserable company for Nick and his family, when we meet up for a meal they have cooked for us at their campsite.

FRUSTRATION! IMPATIENCE!

One look at Gwen's heels this morning tells me that time has not solved the problem and we will have to do something. I had noticed swelling in one hind leg yesterday and now she has it in both. So what now?

During the night I had considered the possibility of having her shod on the hind so that she could go without the chafing of the boots for a longer period of time, and now this seems to be the only solution. We look for farriers, but find only one local man and there is no answer when we try to call. Paul says he has noticed that the owners did their own shoeing in the Equestrian Centre, and when we ask if there is such a place nearby we are told yes, only about 5 kilometres back. So that's it then. We collect Vasco, say farewell to Nick and family and go, but of course nothing is ever as simple as it should be. When we find the stables the owner tells us that she uses a farrier, except that when I try to call him there is no answer. So now we can only bandage up Gwen's heels, make it a short day and head off for Estaing (some 15 kilometres further on), and hope for the best.

Fortunately, all goes reasonably well after this. Gwen seems comfortable and we make good progress until we hit the mother of all steep climbs on the mother of all rocky paths, where we lose boots and the pack saddle slips, but still, somehow, make it to the top. Then the rain starts again and our descent into Estaing is made even more interesting by a car rally that is running straight through the centre of the town. Is there someone up there who really hates us or is this just bad luck? The police have to hold the traffic back for us and the horses snort and stare, but then we see a [10]*chambre d'hôte* off to one side and suddenly the world becomes a great deal more pleasant.

Instead of a field, a slightly eccentric looking, and very deaf woman, directs us to a cow shed at the end of her garden. I think that my French is failing me at first, but after several repetitions and exasperated pointing from her, I understand that we are to go through a door and tie up the horses inside while she calls her son. Cow stalls are not the first place I would choose for our horses, but these are wide, furnished with automatic drinkers and personalised with the names of the cows that must have once lived there (Gwen becomes Leticia). Meanwhile it is raining very heavily, and though it is only early afternoon I am very grateful to Gwen for providing us with an excuse for not going on.

During our ride over, we have been able to speak to the farrier, only to find out at that he will not be available until Wednesday, which means staying in Estaing for four days. This is not what I want to hear, but Paul is more reasonable and when he points out Estaing's claim to be the most beautiful town of the region,

I grudgingly agree. After a good meal we go into a bar for a final drink and find ourselves in the middle of Jean's (our landlord) fiftieth birthday party. We are immediately treated to a glass of champagne each and I decide that things are not so bad after all.

Bags of Pasta

Gwen's hind legs are still swollen and it is worrying, though the good news is that we have the river to bathe them in. Well, this is what I tell Paul the next day, though actually I have very little hope of getting her in there. Nevertheless, we take the gang down and try with Lubie first, who, to my utter amazment, goes in and positively wallows, pawing the water so that we are all soaked. Then, with some minor shoving on my part, Gwen follows too, though Okapi still flatly refuses. Meanwhile, the entire population of Estaing is standing on the bridge to watch us. This will become a daily event, witnessed by similar numbers until we leave.

On our penultimate night, Okapi manages to break his tie and trash all the pack bags. The gas stove is flattened, the kitchen utensils lost somewhere in the straw and a bag of pasta emptied. He has scoffed the lot, plus a packet of granola bars. I watch him closely for the next few hours, because I have no idea what effect dry pasta has on a horse's digestion. Fortunately, in Okapi's case at least, it apparently has none. Then the farrier announces that he will not be arriving until the evening, which adds another day to our unscheduled sojourn in Estaing - five days in all. If this is what people call a character building experience, my character must be about the size of Buckingham Palace by now.

Conques – Where it all started

I have led Jim and Morgan on to grass that made my own mouth water then retired in disgust when they wandered off to a clump of thistles. Jim ate thistle-tops with a lifted head and the expression of a man having a tooth filled.

From These Are My People, by Alan Marshall

During our ride through the area known as the Segala, the landscape is high (about 500 metres), with sudden slashes of deep river valleys. We pass through a series of villages and remote outposts that leave us searching for words and dropping into the inevitable clichés. Some are haunting in their silence; others dominated by churches that belong in cities ten times the size. We hear their bells echoing across the valleys and wonder who they can call in this day and age and in this empty landscape. Then we ride into Conques, too exhausted to appreciate that we have entered the birthplace of our dream that started just twelve months before, almost to the day.

What we need now is good food and accommodation for our horses and a place nearby for us, but the field we are offered by the extremely helpful tourist official is a square of scrubland on sheer mountainside. I watch our bed roll career down the hill and wonder how we can leave our girls on a near vertical slope without any decent grass. Do we have a choice? It seems not. Goats have been there before so why not horses? The enquiry is sincere and I haven't the heart or energy to explain the difference. So we untack the team and slog back down to the hill to the friary where we are going to stay. From there life begins to look up, marginally.

Conques is one of the great villages of southwest France. The houses date from the Middle Ages and have retained all the charm and twisty cobble street mystery that attract tourists in droves. Still, in spite of the overtly sanitising effect of tourism, history hits you with a unsavoury smack here; starting with the cloisters where we are staying. The origins go back to a hermit called Dadon, who settled here sometime in 800AD and founded a community of Benedictine monks, one of whom was not quite as holy as he should have been. In the name of God, presumably, this particular monk pinched the relics of the martyred girl Sainte Foy from the monastery at Agen and brought them to Conques. Dishonest he may have been, but a fool he was not. He guessed that Sainte Foy's presence would bring the pilgrims flocking, earning the abbey a prime place on the pilgrim route and lots of extra land and money from the wealthy and powerful. If he came back now, he'd see that his ruse was more successful than even he could have imagined.

Later we have a meal in front of the Romanesque church of Sainte Foy, but the Last Judgement in its tympanum does not do a lot for our appetites. Hungry as we are the images of hell dominate our thoughts. Do we believe in it? No, not in this very corporeal and tortured form, but the reasons for being sent there are uncomfortably current. Inevitably, the conversation reverts back to the London bombs, their roots in the Iraq war and our own complicity in the act, because we have not taken the time out from our own projects to join other people in its condemnation. After that it's back to the here and now. Our horses. We slog back up the hill at least four times before falling into bed ourselves, each time find them grazing peacefully on the narrow terraces and clearly wondering what all the fuss is about.

The next day begins with a good early start and on the way out we stop for a few thoughtful minutes on the Roman Bridge where our dream really started. It is still hard to believe that we are actually here with our horses. We allow ourselves a mutual pat on the back before starting up the steep ascent out of the Conques valley, named after the shell to reflect its shape. The views are staggering, but Gwen hardly gives me time to enjoy them as she launches herself into the almost vertical gradient. Every dog/horse must have its day and this is hers.

On the way we meet Katrina, a twenty-nine-year-old maths teacher, who seems to be faster than us, which I still find irritating despite all the sensible words. We stop and talk for a while and find out that she is doing the distance - going to Santiago – too. A status that immediately instils a different level of camaraderie. Later on we are cheered by a group of walkers who are having a lunch break, and once again I am amazed by the interest and enthusiasm our horses seem to inspire.

The day's ride is very hard and I can't take a step further when we dismount, mainly because I've strained a muscle in my thigh, but the horses are looking good and roll endlessly in the long grass where we are able to let them go free. Just one problem though, the owner has asked us to tape off the end of the field to protect her new apple trees. We can do this without difficulty, but know it is the proverbial red rag for Lubie. In the morning we find her on the other side, the apple trees untouched but a smug expression all over her beloved equine features.

Babette Gallard

ANGELS

On the following day our intention is to travel to Figeac, on the River Cele, in the Lot region, a name featured in every guide book. We are told we should not miss its unspoilt medieval centre, but I am more focused on the sign that tells us we have only 1271 kilometres to go. Only. My groin strain (I have a long line of bruising down one thigh) twinges and I wonder how I am going to make it to the end of the day, never mind the journey. Then Paul delivers the final blow, by pointing to a distant spot on the horizon to inform me that this is where we are heading. Suddenly, driving in an environmentally unfriendly car becomes infinitely preferable.

In spite of all this, the countryside gives us a great ride and the horses do exceptionally well, especially when we have to go through Figeac, wending their way through streams of traffic and over one very narrow and noisy metal pedestrian bridge. This is an important place in terms of the history of the *Chemin* and part of me wants to stop here, but there is nowhere for the horses and it seems ironic that in a place that has built its commerce on the pilgrim routes to both Rocamadour and Santiago de Compostela, we can't find anywhere to stay. Still, not everything is bad, because on the way out, on either side of the trail, the land softens and the hooves of our horses send crickets and lizards scattering in their wake.

From Figeac all goes well, until we come to the part where our faithful Confraternity of St. James sign painters must have either gone on strike or got bored. The little red and white stripes have suddenly disappeared and all we can see are miles of country lanes with attractive wooden signposts to anywhere but the *gîte* that we have seen a nice picture of in our guidebook. Then, just at the point when we are all most knackered, thirsty and pissed off with being pilgrims, Okapi, being a typical teenager, digs his heels in and leaves me hanging on his lead rein while Gwen refuses to wait. My finger snaps, I wrench my groin, lose my temper and blame Paul for not looking in the book properly. He wisely keeps quiet and then five minutes later we stumble on perhaps the most pleasant *gîte* we have found to date.

The proprietors, Jean and Michel Lefrancois, welcome us into their tranquil valley and show us to a lush field stretching out into a shady haze of green. If there is a heaven, I want it to be like this. Then Jean hands over a hose so that we can wash our poor horses, and says nothing when Paul and I fight over it to get a drink for ourselves first.

The *gîte* is spread through a number of converted barns and outhouses that have been left more or less intact in the local stone, and the gardens only barely tamed. Later, when I find the energy, I take a tour and find that silent areas have been put aside for pilgrims in a contemplative mood. Some will be religious, but I suspect that, like me, the majority are not. Does it matter? Paul is sensitive enough not to search for me until I am ready and then we eat our first meal of the day, during which we meet two Norwegian women, Bjorg and Bannta, and a young Swiss couple, Alexandra and Philippe, who have walked from Lausanne.

Apart from, *Where did you start?* the most common question pilgrims ask each other is: *Have you booked ahead?* How you answer depends on where you are and who you are. In the early stages of our walk we did not book ahead, but now the *Chemin* is filling visibly and we are beginning to think we should. Yes, we could camp, but we also have the horses to consider, well that's our excuse anyway. The truth is that I still haven't got to grips with this thing that the tough people called bivvying, which for me means no shower and sleeping on stone. So, as a means of opening the conversation, we ask Phillipe if he has booked ahead and are surprised when he says he has not, because he looks like the type of sensible Swiss boy who would. Instead, he and Alexandra just smile back beatifically and tell us that they 'Rely on the angels.'

I do a double-take, but his expression has not changed in the interim. Is he serious? Yes, I think he is. The following silence is painful. Those of you reading may be able to think of an obvious and immediate reply, but we could not.

'Angels.' Paul repeats with a slow nod that can be taken to mean anything.

'That's interesting.' I add. 'We just use the mobile.' I was trying to be funny.

An Ocean of Stones

Today we are heading for Cajarc, and congratulating ourselves because we have managed to be on the trail by seven o' clock, until we meet Bjorg and Bannta who have beaten us by an hour. As we travel, we meet a blind man and his partner (Claude and Francois), which prompts a discussion on the degree to which his impressions will differ from ours. I assume that the sounds of the crickets (particularly raucous in this region) will feature, but when Paul comments on the strong scents of pine and turned earth I am reminded that I also suffer a minor form of sensory deprivation myself. I have lost my sense of smell (as a result of the head injury when I was sixteen). From then on I pester him to describe his various olfactory sensations as we proceed. Actually it does not help, because many of them I have never smelt, which means I cannot summon them up in my memory.

We are riding through an 'ocean of stones' and miles of open scrubland that has all the signs of being cultivated in the past, but is now sadly abandoned. The path takes us along the remnants of stone walls, farm houses and small round shepherd shelters (Cazelles) that echo as painfully as the empty shipyards and coalmines of home. Both of us, though we are enjoying the ride, can't help being affected by the sadness of the place. Latterly, the landscape changes to take in shady woodland and small tracks where Gwen becomes a pleasure to ride. Okapi on the other hand is in a particularly bad mood and stops at every opportunity. This makes me think more about our discussions with regard to having a pack pony or not, though for the time being I am determined to succeed, if only because I was the one who insisted we needed him.

After a fairly sticky descent, we come into Cajarc, a large town, surrounded by high red rock cliff faces, pockmarked by caves and in some cases massive caverns. This is also the second place we have passed through (the other being in the Tour des Anglais just outside Aubrac) where the English have left their mark. Here, it is in the form of a crumbling castle set high above the town and built during the Hundred Years War. In another situation we would have spent more time here, but we are on a pilgrimage with three horses and no long-term parking facilities. Paul goes shopping while the equine team takes the opportunity to snatch forty winks. Meanwhile Vasco summons his own personal fan club and is petted and patted until he is heartily sick of it. Sometimes I wonder if being an ordinary, inconspicuous walker would be easier.

In the evening we stay in an equestrian centre in Seuzac, just outside Cajarc, where the horses not only have an enormous field to themselves, but also equine company on the other side of the fence. Okapi struts his stuff while Gwen tries to look coy. Lubie is more interested in stuffing her face and only gives an occasional bum-flash just to show that she really is still a mare. While they socialise, Paul, Vasco and I go swimming in the Lot until the sun goes down.

HEALTH AND PERFORMANCE REVIEW:

Groin strain less painful and less visible

Mileage picking up as we get into the routine and become fitter.

As a result of finding two large ticks on Vasco we have now included the tick check in our morning routine

Vasco has started limping and it looks as if he has broken a claw

EQUIPMENT LOST:

One hammer

Two bottles of shampoo – consecutively

Two pairs of reading glasses – Paul's

One saddle cushion

One digital camera cable - aah!

MISUNDERSTOOD TEENAGER

The target for today is Varaire, and once again we manage an early start, even though the weather is overcast so avoiding the heat is not really an issue. We would have liked to have gone via Saint-Cirq-Lapopie where the famous poet, Andre Breton, lived in the early 1900's, but we both agree that it would add too much to our journey. As always in these situations we make a resolution to go back there some day. The list is growing so fast that we will only achieve this if we add another hundred years to our lives.

The highlight of the day is when we finally find the solution to Okapi's resistance. He just doesn't want to be led. As a last resort I let him go and find that he is much more content and so are we. As a horsewoman I should have realised that my pace with Gwen, and his inexperience, were the root of the problem, but I didn't and I curse myself for the rest of the day.

The terrain is very difficult for our horses, the flint shale so hard to walk on that I begin to ignore the landscape, until Paul mentions that every stone in the walls we are passing has been moved by human hand. A humbling thought. Once again we meet Bjorg and Bannta on the route and agree that we must swap contact details at the next opportunity. Later we are passed by an Austrian who easily outstrips our horses, even when we are intermittently trotting.

On arrival at our *gîte* in the afternoon, Okapi disgraces himself by eating the newly planted herbaceous border, but fortunately for us the woman who owns it does not seem to mind and tells us that it is always being attacked by the donkeys and horses brought by pilgrims. Nevertheless, the accommodation for our equines is 2 kilometres away in another equestrian centre, and when we walk back I realise that my feet are badly out of practice.

Philippe and Alexandra are also staying in the *gîte* and we relate our experience with the amazing

Austrian, but they are already one step ahead, because they had a meal with him the night before. The story is that he has walked from Vienna, averaging 60 kilometres a day, with only a few hours' sleep on a floor somewhere on the way. At first, I am speechless with admiration, but then the truth hits me like a dead cod. Admirable? No, he's insane. We also meet Jean, a Frenchman with blisters the size of tennis balls and not all of them on his feet. I'm confused.

'So where are the others?'

"Ere," he points to a place I definitely don't want to see. "But I have the cream so everything is better now, even my boll-.'

'Got it, Jean.' I raise my hand. Suddenly I don't want to know any more.

Nevertheless, the evening is concluded well with a meal that introduces us to Nicole, Mireille and Guy, three antiquarians who are in business together and clearly very good friends too. They have teamed up with Claude and François on the way and now pull us into their group. Paul and I struggle pathetically with our limited French, but revel in the opportunity to talk with like-minded people, or something like that. In fact, the flowing wine has insured that everyone is beyond comprehension, irrespective of language.

As we go to our dormitory I slur to Paul that this is what being on the *Chemin* is all about, but Jean has another experience in store. He is on a bunk on the other side of the room, sleeping and rumbling, which I can almost forgive, but when he farts Vasco barks with fright. This is the first, though certainly not the last time that I thank fate for taking away my sense of smell.

The next day we start out under a sky full of Simpson clouds. As we set off, the owner of the equestrian centre is very complimentary about Okapi and probably would have bought him on the spot if I had offered to sell. When I take a closer look I can see why, the boy has developed since leaving home. His neck and hindquarters are muscular and he holds himself with a presence that is immediately arresting. I doubt that anyone could have predicted that the hairy little runt we bought just five months ago would turn into such a beautiful equestrian athlete.

ROCK FACES AND BALLET SHOES

On leaving the village we meet Bjorg and Bannta and walk with them, while Vasco makes the best of having his own, exclusive fan club. Bannta has her photo taken with him a number of times and I think took one of us too.

The going is much easier now, with fewer hills, though the path is still very stony. We make good time. On the way, two riders on two large and quite impressive mounts come up behind us and, assuming that they will be much faster, we let them go in front. In fact, it is quite the opposite, but for decorum's sake we try to hold back until they get off to lead their horses when the path becomes mildly more difficult. Now we are forced to pass them and as the gap widens between us, Paul and I conclude that the difference in performance has to be attributed to experience and even more importantly the boots. The grip provided by their plastic soles can only be compared to the tread of a walking boot, and what walker in his or her right mind would tackle a rock face in ballet shoes, something riders expect horses with iron on their feet to do.

In the afternoon we head for the Gîte de Peche, just outside Cahors, and for the first time sleep in our tent, because there are no beds left. At last we are beginning to find a use for it, but the fact that we have managed nearly two weeks without camping at all raises the ugly question again – do we really need a pack pony to carry equipment that is barely used? Clearly, riding with just two horses would be easier, but will we be able to carry everything? An hour is lost while we try to agree on what is vital and what is 'extra', and still the conclusion eludes us, particularly because our tent is just metres away from Okapi who watches us and seems to be listening to every word.

Later, when we join the other pilgrims who had been sensible enough to book a place the day before, we find that most of the crowd from the previous evening are there, excepting Claude and Francois who have stopped off earlier in another *gîte*. Once again we have another memorable evening and feel ourselves drawn into the very specific camaraderie of being pilgrims on a common route with our blisters, aching legs and sunburnt noses.

Hello and Goodbye

Today the horses are having a rest day, but we are not. We need to replace some lost and damaged equipment and decide to walk the 15 kilometres into Cahors, finding on the way that Vasco has hurt a paw, which means we have to carry him. We meet up again with Katrina who tells us that she has had to take a day off further back to recuperate, making me feel better because up to now I thought I was the only one who was feeling so tired. As we walk together we discuss her experience of being a maths teacher in a Parisian suburb, dispelling any pretensions I once had in that direction. She must either be a saint or a masochist to work with kids who spit and throw chairs at their teachers as a form of greeting.

And on the subject of teenagers …. in the centre of Cahors, we meet Nick and Danielle who have been texting us furiously to agree a mutually identifiable place. Once again they have located us on our pilgrim path. I should have known there was something odd going on when Nick said that he had package for me on the back seat of the car, but I'm either infinitely gullible or stupid or both. Anyway, who cares, because it was Lucy, the best present anyone could bring, even if I now have definite proof that I should never believe anything she says, ever again. We hug madly and then go for a beer in a nearby café, where quite by chance we meet Nicole and the rest of the group. The perfect coincidence that is concluded with a picnic in the park and … you guessed, too much wine. Being a pilgrim is tough.

Cahors deserves a closer look, and I have reserved it for the list of places to go back to. In its time it has been ruled by just about everyone, which is obvious from the architecture. Starting out as a Gallic settlement, it went on to become a Roman town, then a Moorish possession and just before it went back to being French, the English got in there with a few years of governance. All good stuff, but this morning my first thought is that we have not managed to meet up with Bjorg and Bannta before they leave Cahors and fly back to Norway. I'm kicking myself and anyone else who gets in my path, and then, as if this isn't bad enough, we have to say goodbye to Nick and family, with Harry crying his heart out, because he has to leave Vasco. Why can't there just be two of everything and everyone? It would be so much easier, though I shouldn't be complaining because I have got all I want. Lucy has decided to stay with us and see how she copes on foot.

After Cahors, we ride on dirt-dry tracks that go on for ever, in an area where horses are trained for endurance riding. Then the landscape pulls back its harsh stone exterior to reveal an underbelly of pure gold, swaying corn and dancing sunflowers, many with smiling faces picked out by passing pilgrims. It's difficult not to feel absolutely privileged and ridiculously happy, even when the sun is beating down like a gas flame on your head.

The horses sweat and for the first time show some susceptibility to the heat. For Lucy the trial is much harder. Thirty kilometres on the first day, without any training or preparation, in shoes designed for pavement mooching. When we arrive at the *Gîte*, Happy Culteur, she is exhausted. I feel utterly responsible, but also totally incapable of doing anything practical to make the process less arduous. I offer to let her ride the next day, but she is adamant that she will walk and I can only stand back in admiration. Which part of the gene pool does this level of stoicism comes from? I can't see a trace of it in either mine or her father's.

The valley of the Happy Culteur cannot go without a mention, because it is probably every English man or woman's image of an earthly Nirvana, a point I make to the owner who only nods wryly in reply. She knows all about the dream, and the work. The organically grown vegetables do not seed themselves, and the water pumped up from the well is not infinite. It's a hard, unforgiving routine, but still I wouldn't mind the chance to give it a try and I'm not alone. Over breakfast we get into conversation with a Swiss guy in his twenties who walked all the way from Geneva. Now he is building a stable for the pregnant donkey, which belongs to the family. He is undecided about his future. A St. James victim and happy to be so.

Then it's more sunflowers, more gold, more suspension of reality until Lubie loses a boot. Pilgrims may have had the brigands, wolves and, on occasion, pestilence to deal with, but they didn't have our expensive plastic boots to send their blood pressure shooting off the scale. While carefully watching Okapi and Gwen, we have fallen into a fall sense of security with Lubie. She has had hardly any problems to date, now they come all at once. A boot gone from her fore without being aware of it, and then another off her hind, which cuts her heel badly. I have visions of another five days waiting while she recuperates and we have to find a farrier. I'm in a bad mood and it hangs over us as we plod on under a baking sun and note the drooping heads of the sunflowers. I know just how they feel. Then, while we stop off for water, a team of pilgrims behind us sees the boots on our horses and realises that this is what they have seen on the path some 5 kilometres back. I'd rather they hadn't said anything at all, because even though we are too tired to retrace our steps now, the fact that the boot is there will rankle for ever. More importantly this means we are dipping into our very limited supply of spares and cannot afford to lose any more.

We plod on and eventually locate the tiny Saint-Sernin chapel where pilgrims past and present have stopped off for a spiritual top-up. In fact, we do not go down the small track that leads to it, because we are looking for the nearby *gîte*. A classic French farmhouse, enhanced by pale pink evening light and a particularly well preserved [11]pigonerie of which we have already bought postcards. Not so bad, and now I am glad we made the effort to go that little bit further, but the joy is short-lived.

First we have to go through the usual opening sequence in bad French:

Bonsoir. Do you have any rooms? Do you take horses? Good, because we have three. No, I'm serious, three. Two for riding and one for the luggage. How many people? Three. No, I know I said two horses for riding, but my daughter is walking with us. Yes, she really does want to.

Then we are shown to a sparse square of land. I'd like to say you must be joking, even though I know it is impolite and a waste of time. Since starting out on the Chemin we have learned that the guidebook slogan, Horses welcome, can indicate facilities ranging from a lush field to a tethering pole next to a house, but this is the worst we have encountered so far. I try to look as if we are not too disappointed, but the poor woman is clearly upset by my reaction and desperate to make amends.

'You can put them anywhere you like,' she tells us, pointing vaguely in the direction of the fields around. 'I own all of it. Twenty hectares.'

This sounds better, but the land, all twenty hectares of it, looks pretty much the same – just dry, unappetising scrubland. Nevertheless, we spot a copse of trees and agree that we can erect some sort of fence inside it. The only problem is that we have to lug their water over a distance of 100 metres and my groin strain is back with a vengeance. Who said that riding down the St. James Way would be fun? We put the bells on Lubie and Okapi and hope for the best. Meanwhile, poor Lucy has slogged another 30 kilometres and is literally in tears with exhaustion by the time she reaches the *gîte*. I suggest she rides and she refuses. Instead she has agreed to try Paul's sandals and

SOCKS. I know from this, just how bad things must be for her.

Later, while Paul and I walk back after delivering yet another bucket of water to our ever-thirsty horses, we meet an elderly couple and strike up a conversation about the area. They tell us that the house we are staying in used to belong to a very well-known sculptor and his wife, but that they had been killed in a plane crash the previous year. The woman we had met was their daughter and the only one left living in the house. She is struggling. In the darkness, I sense Paul's eyes search mine. If only I had known …

In the morning we meet more formally a woman we had seen only briefly the night before. Paul goes over to speak to her in the first instance and finds out that she is Austrian. She will be referred to as the Austrian woman for days after, though this morning we don't have time to talk because suddenly Mireille and Guy are on the road outside. It's seven o'clock and they have already been walking for an hour - a fortuitous meeting that is like the proverbial gift from heaven. We greet and part in the space of five minutes, but promise to meet up and exchange addresses when we reach Moissac.

HEALTH AND PERFORMANCE REVIEW:

Gwen showing clear signs of weight loss.

Needing to dress Lubie's heel though it is healing well.

Okapi has a rub from one of the boot straps - not serious.

My groin strain is making any kind of movement painful and mounting impossible without something to stand on.

Both Paul and I still feel very tired after a day's riding.

Blisters rising like angry mountains all over Lucy's feet

PILGRIMS

It was midsummer, and the absence of water along the road began to worry us. Late as it was, we kept hoping to find some dam beside which we could camp.

From These Are My People, by Alan Marshall

The landscape continues to soften as we progress. The *Chemin* alternates between wonderfully shady paths through large expanses of woodland and rolling hills exposed to the fierce sun. Everything is dust-dry. The horses are continually desperate for water, but the troughs that were so frequent at the beginning are now in very short supply. I scour the hillsides for the cemeteries that are frequently equipped with taps. In the end we stop at a public lavatory where a woman is made to wait while Gwen has her nose plunged in the sink. This kind of behaviour is not good PR for future equestrian pilgrims, so Paul tracks down an English family who kindly offer us a hose and endless water. Resourcefulness is one of his greatest skills.

For the humans in the team, sustenance is not quite so hard to find now that we are walking through endless orchards and some wild fruit trees I presume have planted themselves. Frustratingly, the majority (particularly the wild figs!) are not yet ripe, but the apricots are, so we scrump some and buy a few kilos more from a farmer who gives the horses water too. Lucy also manages to find some melons that have been left in the verge, with a note saying pilgrims should take what they want.

"See, it's like I told you." I say enthusiastically. "Walking on the St. James Way is not just like doing the Pennine Way or Offa's Dyke, it's a spiritual experience and you are assigned a higher status by the people who live here."

'Tell that to my feet.' She responds.

Trust a teenager to shatter my dreams.

In the afternoon, Lucy finally agrees to ride and we enjoy trotting alongside each other, something we have not been able to do properly since her old pony developed chronic [12]laminitis. Meanwhile, Paul is on foot leading Okapi and wearing his shorts, sandals and socks. He looks more like a scoutmaster than a pilgrim.

In Moissac, Lucy and I make our way through lines of impatient traffic and thundering lorries, only stopping once when a man crosses the road to shake our hands and make us feel inordinately privileged. Finally, we reach a refuge run by nuns from the Carmelite Order. In memory of my unpleasant experience of being a boarder in a school run by Catholic nuns, I am ready to hate everything and everyone I see there, but we are greeted charmingly and assured that there are good facilities for horses. I breathe a sigh of relief and enjoy a pleasant walk up to the top of their exquisitely landscaped garden, envisaging a lush, well fenced meadow at its peak.

'This? You mean here?'

The nod and smile I receive in reply is beneficent. 'We knew you would be pleased. Our pilgrims always are.'

What can I say in the face of such genuine zeal? Clearly the belief is that our horses will be just like the donkeys they are used to receiving, and so this patch of scraped soil will be more than ample. How could they know that a member of our equine team is genetically linked to Houdini?

With no other alternative, Lucy and I set about rigging up a tape enclosure for Okapi and Gwen, with a separate tether line for Lubie. In the interim Paul walks on behind and manages to negotiate the delivery of a sack of feed, much to their delight and, thankfully, a distraction from eating the trees.

My father always used to say that you can only appreciate happiness if you have unhappiness as a comparator. As a teenager I rated this as just more of the usual adult twaddle, but the *Chemin* has repeatedly proved him right. Simple things like a shower at the end of a hard day can wash away the sweat and ease aching muscles. Meeting friends puts you entirely back on your feet. Having scraped off the grime and put on some relatively clean clothes, Paul, Lucy and I saunter contentedly into the plaza in front of Moissac's slightly bizarre (in my view), but very famous abbey of St-Pierre. We are looking for a beer, then find Mireille and Guy.

I am not used to events working out the way I want, but if there is a deity who decides on this kind of thing, he/she must have been in a good mood that day or thought we deserved a break. Anyway, everything is absolutely perfect, right down to the very finest detail, because they have just decided that this is to be their last day on the Chemin. We immediately exchange addresses and arrange to meet later for the communal evening meal, an inevitably lengthy and wine-laden event during which there are fond farewells and promises to meet up later. Sometimes life is just good, plain good.

HEALTH AND PERFORMANCE REVIEW:

Gwen's weight loss is now obvious and worrying, though the others are showing hardly any signs. Nevertheless, comments from people seem to indicate that our horses are not doing badly in comparison with others they have seen. For example, a Swiss couple had to leave their pony behind because it couldn't cope with the heat, and an English woman we spoke to said that our horses looked very fit compared to others that were clearly run down. Maybe we are doing something right.

Okapi still going much better since we took him off the lead rein – poor misunderstood chap – I can leave him loose on small roads without any fears, unless we pass a maize field where his stomach will take over.

Rubs from the boots still needing attention on Lubie.

Fur, Feather and Wings

Riding along the St. James Way is a mixture of highs and lows and today is no exception. The landscape is just as Mireille had promised (and she should know because she did the entire length in 2002), there are no more hills and our causeway walk between the Garonne River and canal is shaded by massive plane trees. This is tranquil, flat and easy riding that gives us time to think and talk. What a change from the last few days, though it is still very hot. At lunch time we flop out on the grassy banks, while the horses gorge on lush grass. This is good. I hum Summertime in my head, but of course good times can't go on for ever.

The first change comes when a fledgling flops across our path. It can't fly and we are worried that it will be hurt, so in best tradition Paul gets off to move it, except that the bird doesn't understand and flies pathetically into the water.

We watch uselessly from the side as it sinks and progressively fails. I don't know what to do. Should I throw myself into the water and rescue it? Would that help? The bird hasn't got time to wait while I search my soul and within the space of seconds it has drawn its last breath in front of our eyes. All three of us stare silently at each other, but there is nothing to say. We meant well. How many other people have said that?

Next, a minor and far more positive diversion crosses our path when we see a pilgrim taking a rest in the shade, reading a book with a tiny kitten in her lap. We don't stop because it seems a shame to disturb the tranquil scene, but we speculate on how the kitten had got there. Had she found it here or brought it with her? Did she travel with it all the time?

Then we leave the shaded banks of the canal and come out into the sun, a sensation akin to walking into a microwave on full power. Worse still, we are slogging on roads that leap over perpendicular hills at all too regular intervals and Lucy is back on foot. We call on the mobile to check her progress, and hear that she is surprisingly fit and keen to go on, because she has teamed up with the Austrian woman, Annaliese. Good company makes the going a great deal easier.

In Auvillar – a beautiful town with a circular and columned corn market in the middle and honey stone buildings – Paul tells me to try to sniff out the scented soap made there, but my intermittent olfactory senses are on strike, and even though the smell is apparently overpowering it still eludes me. As we travel we are stopped (even more than usual) by people wanting to take photos, which makes me horribly self-conscious. The others who wave from cars and sometimes clap or cheer from their windows are easier to cope with.

As the afternoon progresses and the heat increases, we agree that there is no way we can push on to the equestrian centre we had been aiming for, and decide to try a *gîte* in the tiny village of St. Antoine, even though there is no mention of it taking horses. As we walk through, we ask at the restaurant if there are any places to put them and are told, no problem, the *gîte* is an old farm and has facilities. This is good news and an indication that maybe we don't have to rely quite so slavishly on the information given in our guide book.

When we get there we are greeted by an exceptionally friendly old couple who can't do enough to help. The problem is that the horse accommodation they so enthusiastically take us to is just a tether post in a patch of ground, between an array of old farming implements. By this time, we have developed the art of hiding our horror, but we still have to explain that one tether post simply isn't enough for three horses. Thankfully, the old man takes this well and is happy to help us rig up an enclosure with our white tape, even going to the trouble of making up a few more metal posts to support it. We are effusive in our thanks and, after feeding the horses, sink exhausted on to a bench next to Annaliese and Lucy who have just walked in.

Our beer isn't even half drunk when the whinnying starts. Something is obviously wrong and when I go to investigate, I find Gwen tethered to the post and pouring with sweat. What has happened? She is covered in coin sized swellings that can only be insect bites. What insect could produce a reaction this severe? As I examine her the old man comes to tell me that she has jumped out of the enclosure and trampled over his garden. This is awful and of course I apologise profusely, but I am more worried about what made her do it.

Back at the enclosure the answer is all too obvious. Hornets, swarms of them that attack me as I come near. I've never seen anything like it and dive through the maddened cloud to get the other horses out. On the way vicious sharp bursts of pain tell me that I am being stung, but everything is happening too fast to change my mind. At the same time Madame has come out with a spray can and is blasting at the beasts as we try desperately to avoid them. The air is full of the toxic stuff and I'm not sure which is worse, the insects or the spray, but one thing I do know – we have got to get the horses away.

During our previous discussion with the restaurateur, I had heard him mention that there was also a piece of communal ground that might be available for the horses if the *gîte* could not accommodate us, so now we race back up to the restaurant to explain the situation and ask for help. It is immediately forthcoming, in the form of water, much stale bread (for the horses), lots of interested sympathy and more importantly a call to the *Monsieur le Maire* who apparently promises to sort something out. In fact, he arranges an alternative place in our current landlord's hay field – such generosity – just one problem – no fences and it is some 500 metres away from the *gîte*. Beggars can't be choosers, so Lucy and I slog down there with the horses, while Paul does his best to build a Lubie-proof fence.

Half an hour later, we think we have done all that is required and stumble over to the restaurant. Are we too late to be served? Not at all, we are told kindly, except that before we sit down we might like to collect our horses that have just been spotted in a maize field.

I could scream, or simply break down in tears, but it would be a waste of time and that is something we don't have. The horses are eating a farmer's maize, which could be expensive, embarrassing and bad press for any other riders coming in our wake. Lucy and I race off in one direction and Paul in another. We search, see nothing, and then finally catch a glimpse of a dark shape in a distant corner of the village. A horse? Or is that Paul waving madly at us? Both actually, because he is standing with the horses in someone's garden.

Incredibly, the owners don't seem to mind. In fact, they're laughing by the time we get there and joke that Gwen wouldn't drink the cocktail she was offered. This is too good to be true. Is St. Antoine real or are we in some kind of heaven's nightmare? There is even better to come.

Just as we are debating what to do next with our wild horses, a woman crosses the road and asks if we would like to put them in her garden for the night. We view the carefully tended trees, the swimming pool and herbaceous borders. Is she sure? Absolutely, and her husband is quite insistent, because he loves all animals. Is this one of your angels, Philippe?

Paddling pools and sand pits are emptied to give the horses drinking water. Pots are pulled out of the way and no one objects to our tying the tether rope between two fruit trees. The children want to pat Lubie, but she is stressed and won't play the game. How do you thank such kindness? I try to set off the preliminaries by asking the husband's name, but he tells me that his name is of no importance, because he is just happy to help. We leave speechless, dazed and oh so-ooo-oo relieved.

ANOTHER ST. JAMES VICTIM

Today we are late starting, because we've a great deal of tidying up to do, plus the horses are now being driven crazy by swarms of persistent flies. Gwen looks as if someone has been firing golf balls under her skin, but we have to go on because another episode like the previous one could be the death of us all. Why Gwen? My unfortunate Gwen who seems to attract every disaster of the most unattractive nature. If she were a human she would have acne, eczema and flat feet.

The weather is overcast and uncomfortable, but the ride is mercifully uneventful through gentle rolling hills. Lucy walks with Annaliese until we get to Lectoure, a pretty medieval town built on a high ridge, where we intend to stay, though Annaliese decides to go on. We say our goodbyes with promises to stay in touch, even though our minds are on another difficulty – our guide book does not mention any places that take horses here and we don't have the energy to go on. Lucy is given the task of going to the Tourist Office to ask if there are any fields in the area and, in spite of being exhausted herself, she manages to locate one just outside the town. This is a very real success and yet another sign that we do not have to rely slavishly on the guide book.

Tonight we are staying in a *gîte* that has just been opened by Isabelle, a young woman from Paris who walked the [13]*Camino* in Spain last year, and consequently decided to change her life by giving up her job and moving out, yet another St. James victim. The house she has chosen is perfect and she has used every corner to best advantage. I feel a twinge of envy as we look round, and then the evening is made even more memorable when a French woman we have spoken to over the past few days, starts to sing some traditional French folk songs. Later, over a communal dinner, comments are made about the small number of English seen on the Chemin, something we cannot explain. Then another pilgrim tells us what we most want to hear – travelling in Spain is easy, perhaps even easier than in France, because the *gîte*s are better organised and water more frequently available.

HEALTH AND PERFORMANCE REVIEW:

Okapi is showing signs of sore heels

All horses are showing scuffs from the ordeal in St. Antoine and are covered in silver antiseptic spray.

Gwen looks like a robot.

Gwen's bites are still bad, but showing no signs of breaking under the saddle – my greatest fear.

All – horses, humans and kit - are showing signs of fatigue - how can we last for another 1000 kilometres?

Paul and I are now seriously considering how we can manage without a pack pony – we are hoping to arrange for Ray to pick up Okapi just before we tackle the Pyrenees.

INCLEMENT WEATHER

Once again a beautiful ride through rolling fields of corn and sunflowers. The combine harvesters are hard at work and many fields have already been cut. In contrast to the places we have been through only a week before, there is a noticeable lack of livestock in these dry plains. Progress in the heat is a struggle for all of us and Lucy has to ride the second half of the day, with Paul walking behind.

As we reach Condom, the traffic doubles in volume and the lorry drivers seem hell-bent on pushing us off the side of the road. The horses cope well, though Gwen is noticeably tired and I worry, because this could be a sign that the hornet stings are having a more serious effect than I had initially thought. We agree that the next day will be a rest day and manage to negotiate a field for them in a camp site.

It has shady places, good hay and as much hard feed as we can stuff down them in forty-eight hours. This is when I discover that the bite on Gwen's back has opened. Great care will be needed from now on.

The next day we saunter around the town and try to discover some of the very strong pilgrim past, but find that in spite of starting off in the 11th century with a Benedictine abbey and establishing several pilgrim hospitals in the 14th century, Condom's main focus today seems to be on the rubber item that has nothing to do with the place anyway. We don't have the energy or enthusiasm to go to the small 'c' museum because we have already exhausted ourselves and all the jokes. Instead, we do some vital shopping, visit a laundrette (really clean socks and knickers - I'm in heaven), send a few emails and then prepare to walk back. Just as we are about to leave I feel a soft tap on my shoulder. 'Macht's gut.'

Only one person speaks German to me here and I know straight away that it is Anneliese. She has found us to say goodbye. I had half expected it, but still feel very sorry to see her go. Anneliese has slogged along endless stony tracks under a baking sun, keeping up a jogger's pace the whole way, but the *Chemin* is no fun for a mountain walker from Vienna, and she has finally decided to call a halt. Lucy, who has shared much of her pain, is invited to visit her whenever she wants, while we promise to keep in touch. You meet all sorts on the *Chemin* - some are just better than others.

Back at the campsite we doze for the rest of the afternoon until another group of what Lucy generically dubs the Happy Clappies, punctures our tranquillity. It's not the first time we have met this particular group and because we know what's coming our patience is short. We have been irritated by their overt joviality, driven into the ditches by their transport, crushed in kitchens by their cooks and driven mad by their warbling with religious overtones. Are we being unfair? Probably, but it's just one of those situations where you have to be there to understand.

This particular group has back-up like no other. A twenty seater van following them at every stage to pick up the weary and delivering lunches that are spread tantalizingly across our path. We whine that this is not pilgrimming in the terms we understand, but perhaps it's their singing we really object to. I try to smile and hide my feelings when we meet, while refusing to initiate any kind of conversation or apologise when Paul reminds me that this not the way a pilgrim should behave.

The thunder increased in intensity. It was directly overhead. The shattering cracks ripped towards the earth and burst in blinding flashes that seemed only a few feet above the ground. They were not the rumbling peals I was familiar with ... the wind howled and screeched, tearing first from one quarter, then suddenly veering and coming furiously from another.

From These Are My People, by Alan Marshall

No doubt, because Noah's flood and all that are already on my mind, (it had to be the fault of the Happy Clappies in some way) I begin to feel nervous when the owner of the campsite warns Lucy that there is bad weather on the way, and we should put our tent in the barn. Five minutes later the heavens open, dropping a thunderbolt directly on our heads – perhaps a sign I should take note of. Paul and I know we should go out to the horses and manage a couple of dashes out into the blinding rain, but in fact there is little we can do. 'Perhaps the rain will be good for Gwen's stings.' I reason, before sticking my head back in my sleeping bag. What a coward.

Today, we are riding in the intense post-storm heat, with Gwen seeming uncomfortable, though after checking her back I can't see any signs that it is worsening. Scanning the views, I notice we have moved out of the sunflowers and into vineyards, some newly planted, which Paul and I conclude is strange in view of that fact that France is already overproducing wine.

As we ride, we meet up with Phillipe and Alexandra again, though we had assumed they must be days ahead of us by now. It's good to see them and they seem surprisingly pleased to see us, not only because we are such wonderful people, but also because they apparently enjoy tracking our progress by gauging the freshness of our horses' droppings (they are not the only pilgrims to tell us this – probably going back to a Davie Crockett film they have seen). In addition to this clue, they had also met Annaliese who had told them that we were in the vicinity, thus proving the efficacy of the pilgrim network.

The day was sultry, but it became worse after lunch. Dark clouds were gathering and lightening on the horizon. There were rumbles of thunder. In the east a strange, dark cloud streaked earthward as if tipping tons of water on the bush away across the flat paddocks.

From These Are My People, by Alan Marshall

Not long after, a call comes through on our mobile. Rachel (an English woman we had met while staying just outside Cahors) is phoning to tell us that a storm warning has gone out to all the *Mairies* across this part of the country. We are grateful for her thoughts on our behalf and note that the sky is already an ominous pewter colour, but the day ends uneventfully and we find good accommodation in an old and long closed equestrian centre. Then the storm hits, with hail stones clattering like pebbles on the roofs around us and trees bent horizontally in front of the wind. This time I do go out to check on the horses, but find them grazing and obviously unperturbed. After all, they've seen it all before.

Not surprisingly, after what has been chucked at us over the past few days, the weather dominates our thoughts and I note that today it is cool and still cloudy, which makes walking and riding easier. We are moving into lush countryside that rolls out before us in stark contrast to the parched fields we have been riding through until now, but the thin layer of water has left the soil slick and greasy and the horses skate nervously on the mildest of slopes. When I hear a thump behind me I know without looking that Lubie has gone down. Thankfully, Paul is thrown clear and no one is hurt. We reflect that this is only his second fall to date, not bad going for a rider of less than six months.

In Nogaro, otherwise known as 'what has this place got to do with pilgrimages', because we can't see a church or anything remotely pilgrim-like, we arrive at a *gîte d'etape* where we are told there is no room for us and no facilities for the horses (in spite of the horses welcome claim in our guide book). Perhaps I should have stuffed a pillow up my tee-shirt and claimed Gwen was just a rather large donkey, but where there is a will there is a way and we have a tent, so we are allowed to camp on a patch of green nearby and tether the horses to a concrete fence. Then, having set up, we take a walk round the town and find ourselves on the edge of a Formula 2 race track, where trainee Renault drivers are being put through their paces. A bizarre spectacle after our slow progress on the *Chemin*. I watch their frenetic, circular progress to nowhere and feel completely divorced from the world we left only twenty-eight days before.

In spite of all this, meeting people is one of the major perks of the St. James experience, and over the evening meal we strike up a conversation with a middle-aged couple who have walked all the way from Leipzig and are 'doing the distance' to Santiago. I am speechless with admiration, but it doesn't end there, because later we meet Irene from Holland who has walked over 2000 kilometres from her home, and won't be stopping until she falls off the edge of the world in Finisterre.

Over a bottle of local hooch given to us by another pilgrim, Irene tells us that she needs time out to decide what she wants to do next after finishing her degree. We also learn that she is the girl we have seen with the kitten on the banks of the Garonne canal, an amazing fact that finally closes the circle on this story. The kitten had been abandoned, but Irene had rescued it and they had travelled together for some weeks before the heat became too fierce and she found another alternative. Now it is travelling back to Holland, where it will stay with a friend until she returns and is able to look after it herself. A happy ending.

Vandals

I remember hearing a thump in the middle of the night, though in the darkness couldn't see nothing untoward. In the morning light the scene is very different. Two concrete poles and their rails are lying in a crumpled heap on the ground and Lubie is (thankfully) still tethered to them.

Paul's initial reaction is to get out as fast as we can, and I almost go along with him until Lucy in her teenage wisdom tells us that we can't behave so irresponsibly and must face the music. We know she is right, and should be the ones setting a good example, so we ask her to write a note in French, explaining the situation, promising to pay for the damages and including our mobile number. Then we get the hell out.

Later the mobile rings. I have been dreading this moment, but know there is no choice. I have to answer it. The voice at the other end speaks fast, too fast for my poor French, a problem further exacerbated by Gwen who is stamping impatiently under me.

'Did you leave the note?'

'Yes, I'm really sorry, I will pay- '

'Don't worry.'

'Sorry, I didn't quite understand, could you repeat- '

'No problem. Have a good trip.'

'But - '

'Goodbye.'

We thank Phillipe's Angels (just in case they do exist), breathe a huge sigh of relief and set about putting as much distance as we can between our horses and concrete posts.

We are leaving the vineyards to enter a different type of landscape, though it is still lush and rich. Lucy is walking with Irene and I am pleased, because in spite of their age differences they appear to get on extremely well and their conversation will inevitably help the distance to pass.

On the way a dog, even smaller than Vasco, teams up with us and refuses to be put off. We ask various people if they know it, and everyone denies all knowledge, so we seem to have no alternative but to let it follow. Vasco seems content with the arrangement too, at least until the other dog steals part of our lunch and so his share of it.

Towards the end of our day the track takes us into deep woodland that has only been barely cleared. The horses have to negotiate fallen logs and low hanging branches, and today Okapi is the star. Without any guidance or lead from me, the little chap faces every challenge without a pause, jumping in and out of ditches and squeezing the fat packs between narrowly spaced trees. This is where he performs best and I have images of him doing the same with a young girl or boy on his back. Much more fun than being a pack pony for us.

As we come back on to the road I hear a metallic ring and see one of Gwen's hind shoes lying in her wake, as thin as tin foil after only three weeks of use, the last two of which were on relatively soft terrain. Proof, if proof were needed, that in this situation the plastic boots are by far the better option. Nearly 800 kilometres in, and the soles are only showing minor signs of wear, whereas with iron shoes we would have been forced to look for a farrier every three weeks and with the horses' hooves suffering accordingly.

Today we stay in a *gîte* where horses are most definitely welcome and well provided for too. As we enter the yard, I see a Shetland pony and donkey roaming free in the orchard beyond, but we are shown to a field that has everything we and our hard-pressed equines could desire – a fence, a shelter, some grass and a large trough of water. So maybe they have to share all of this with a herd of sheep, but neither side seems to mind.

Of course nothing can ever go entirely according to plan, and less than half an hour later the idyllic scene shatters when Madame leaves the gate open while hanging out the washing. This is when we discover that both the Shetland and the donkey are stallions, a situation that is more or less irrelevant when they are on their own, but one that changes radically when two mares appear on the scene. The Shetland is first in and all hell is let loose. Some say that size does not matter and he would probably agree, Lubie does not. She takes one look at the runt and lets fly with her hooves. This is looking dangerous. Then Gwen weighs in with Okapi in hot pursuit.

I scream for Paul and then *Monsieur* comes in for good measure with a stick. Someone with a camera could have had a great time, because it must have been a hysterical sight. Three horses and something marginally larger than a dog, racing round the field and never meeting in the middle. It takes only twenty minutes to separate them, even though it feels like an hour, and then just as we are breathing a sigh of relief, the donkey slips in. I used to think they were cute, now I know that they are just little grey fiends from hell. And let's not forget our canine stowaway, now known as Basie, thanks to Irene. Lucy is applying the pressure for us to keep him and my only plausible argument against is that he has a flea collar and seems reasonably well looked after. 'Somewhere out there is a distressed owner frantically looking for him,' I protest, but it doesn't really matter what I say because Paul has already invited him onto his lap.

We discuss the options with our very friendly *gîte* owners and they tell us that there is a dog rescue organisation in the nearby town, though of course, as fate would have it, it is Saturday evening. We try phoning the *gendarmerie,* but receive little help, other than the suggestion that we call the dog rescue place. So, after a very pleasant evening meal, during which the owners present us with two bottles of wine and refuse payment, Basie comes to bed with us and pushes poor Vasco out to sleep with Lucy.

LAND OF THE LIVING

The day starts with good news – the wonderful *gîte* family will take Basie to the dog's home on Monday, so now we can leave knowing that we have given him and his owner a chance to find each other. If not, I have promised Lucy that we will come back to get him.

We are having another, very pleasant riding day, not too hot and through rolling fields filled with livestock – a living landscape at last. Vasco, meanwhile, has rediscovered the joys of riding and asks to be picked up whenever we stop. I don't mind, because he needs to conserve his strength and his claw still seems to be sore. He has also sorted out his position across the pack roll and now rides astride like us, rising to the trot and looking like the proverbial nodding dog.

As the riding becomes easier, we are able to free our minds as we had hoped and even take time out to stop off at some of the chapels on the way. Lucy seems to be deriving some benefit too and during her walking with Irene discusses a vast range of esoteric themes: theosophy, our role in the world as individuals and the shape of her own future, being just three of the examples she gives me. In the evening I dismount and realise that I must be getting fitter because I am not aching. The horses seem less tired too, even though we are including some quite long stretches of trotting on the way. This is progress.

Tonight's *gîte* in Arzacq-Arraziguet is less pleasant for the horses because they are strung up between two poles on a flat expanse of field that has been left to weeds. The good news is that there is a feed shop nearby, meaning we are able to stuff them with concentrates and take their minds off the inevitable boredom. When we wake to rain the next day we decide that we might as well stay and make this our seventh day. For Lucy this means saying goodbye to Irene, because it is unlikely we will meet up again before Lucy goes back home, but Paul and I hope to meet her later, perhaps in time for crossing the Spanish border.

Overnight, the horses have wound themselves into a cat's cradle, though they don't panic and simply wait for us to come and sort them out. As we fiddle around a woman with a donkey arrives and tethers it to a post next to ours. Seeing this I realise how easy dealing with donkeys is and why so many people cannot understand what horses need. I try to meet the woman later to speak to her, but she is elusive. Perhaps she has had enough of pilgrims. Once again, we meet the couple from Leipzig. She is now suffering quite badly and takes the bus from time to time, while he walks on. We discuss their stoicism and note that in spite of the hardships, the concept of giving up has never entered their heads. Later, we take a look in the church and find a map full of pins stuck in by pilgrims to show their origin - a visual image of the incredible drawing power of the St. James Way. There are pins in China, Russia, DRC and other equally remote (in European terms) and unexpected countries. What motivates all these people to come here? Surely it can't all be religious fervour? Pins crowd and jostle for space in France, Spain, Germany and the Scandinavian countries. Interestingly the number in Britain is surprisingly low, which bears out our own experience. Why? Is it simply due to a lack of information or worse, a lack of interest?

AN ATTACK OF BUCOLIA

Today Paul announces that he has is having an attack of bucolia. The vistas of gentle, verdant hillsides, dotted with small villages and even smaller farmsteads prompting him to spout the few lines of poetry he knows and burst into song, while Lubie plods on and feigns indifference. For my part, I notice that now the houses are made of rounds stones, instead of the sharp limestone wedges we have been seeing recently.

We stop off at a number of churches, one of which has a memorial to a family that lost six sons in the First World War. I wonder if the men women and children from all sides lost since the start of the Iraqi war will receive the same recognition. Probably not. At another church we sit for a time and then leave as a group of German Happy Clappies enters. Just as we are remounting the sound of a flute drifts over to us and we realise that it is coming from the church. We stay for another half hour, listening and making use of the one thing we have in abundance, time.

From some remote embrace the sky and mountains parted. Pale and exhausted, the dividing range detached itself from a bed of blue and stood erect upon the horizon.

We watched it gain in strength, increase in size. From pale blue to sea blue, to from sea blue to tawny green.

From These Are My People, by Alan Marshall

As we ride, the Pyrenees slink into the horizon ahead, grey slugs of shadow that seem to grow with every step. In Arthez-de-Béarn, we eat an ice cream and stare silently into the distance. Is that really where we are going with our horses? And can we believe the sign that says we have only got 953 kilometres to go?

In the *gîte d'etape* we are shown to a lush field previously untouched by equines. Ours get a whiff of the grass and are beside themselves with excitement, but first they have to get through a narrow door and down a flight of steep steps. We untack them so that they can fit through.

Paul goes with Lubie first, because she is the most sensible. Okapi next, because he is the smallest.

Then it's time for Gwen who just looks at me and sighs.

Gwen: Do you really expect me to get through that?

Me: Well, I'd like you to give it a try.

Gwen: Sigh ... here goes then ... don't blame me if it all goes wrong.

We take our courage in our hands and hooves and launch ourselves with the inevitable results. I am mangled and predictably, Gwen loses control of her bowels, but we are still alive and more or less in one piece when we reach the last stair, so I count it as a success.

With the horses put to bed, Paul and I get down to practicalities. Okapi will go back and Lucy will go with him because she has to prepare for *Lycée*. We phone Ray and he helpfully agrees to fit in with our plans. We arrange a date and place, fixing our own and Okapi's future once and for all. We will go on without a pack pony and he will not be one in the future. I think we all feel better for having made the decision.

Next day, and disaster. Lucy has lost her contact lenses. I curse and stomp, but it doesn't help. Nothing will change the fact that she cannot see without them. What can we do? I trawl through all the alternatives and then notice the Happy Clappies from Germany we had heard playing in the church. I put on my most hypocritical smile, approach the man who appears to be the leader and explain the situation. He is charming and immediately agrees to let Lucy walk with them. Just one problem. I have been able to speak to them in German, but Lucy cannot and their English is minimal. My still smouldering irritation with her carelessness tells me that it serves her right. When I can see that she is close to tears, I agree to wait and meet up with her so that she can ride Lubie, while Paul walks on ahead.

From here the rest of the day proceeds well. Lubie, in her role as Paul's guide, now does the same for Lucy and being unable to see is clearly not a problem. We negotiate some major roads, swim in a shallow river, scramble up some steep slopes, which I presume are a forewarning of the Pyrenees to come, then end up in Naverrenx, where Paul has negotiated a place for us on a campsite and a square of turf for the horses outside. It is far from ideal, but perfect when nothing else is available and we are grateful to the English couple who allowed it.

Now we are in the Basque region, where every road sign is dually translated, and the houses are painted white with red shutters. The three Basque provinces share a common language and refer to their country as Euskal-herri: a land in itself. The indefinably different atmosphere is immediately noticeable and appealing. The distances grow between townships and the *Chemin* loops between valleys and peaks while the Pyrenees grow larger in front. As we approach the small village of Aroue, where we have nominally booked a place, we pass a farm where the facilities for horses appear to be better than those described on the phone when we booked, so we stop and ask if there is space. The answer is initially negative, because all the beds are full, but we must have looked pathetic, or maybe it was the heat or Gwen's hang-horse look, because just as we are turning round to go the owner takes pity on us and suggests we pitch our tent in the field with the horses. Then Irene walks up the road and completes the picture, with a two-metre-high bamboo cane stuck in her rucksack and a filthy cold that I hope she won't pass on.

The evening meal (prepared by our hostess's mother) is excellent, most of it made from the produce of the farm and arriving in plate-bending quantities. The company is exceptional too and this is what we will remember most. Some we know already from nodding and exchanging a few words on route: the French couple who tell Lucy that wearing contact lenses will make her blind and the French trio, (two women and a man), who collapse with helpless laughter every time they see Vasco riding. Others are new, but most come from the German Happy Clappy group and after their kindness to Lucy, I try to be friendly. The leader (a priest, as I find out later) explains the group's motives and aims for being on the St. James Way, while I eat a large helping of humble pie and swallow a bellyful of prejudices. The group has been meeting for seven years already, joining from the prior parishes of the priest in all corners of Germany to complete a small section of the route each. They do so for a variety of personal reasons, some of which include religion or, more often I think, as an incidental factor in a life-changing experience that has left them off-balance and in need of support. The term Happy Clappies drops out of use, for tonight at least.

HEALTH AND PERFORMANCE REVIEW:

Horses are much fitter, trotting frequently and launching themselves up hills without a breather.

One of Gwen's hind heels looking worn – worrying

Gwen's back still not healed, but I hope that if I keep it protected it will be fine. Lucy has done another 30 kilometres without any great pain – she is getting fitter too

LOSSES:

Numerous socks – I hold Lucy entirely responsible.

Contact lenses

My beloved Don Quixote book

In spite of the wine, we spend a sleepless night in the tent, principally because the horses insist on eating grass, noisily, next to our tent. Why when they have a whole field to feed in? Then we get up to discover that Okapi has trashed our tack, destroyed and sucked out the inside of Irene's bamboo cane and eaten a whole bag of Vasco's dog food. I don't bother with worrying about his digestion.

Lucy walks with Irene again.

FOOTHILLS OF THE PYRENEES

Today is hot and we are beginning to feel the tilt of the Pyrenees, with even Gwen slowing down. As we climb, we are alternately transfixed by vistas of panoramic views or plunged into valleys of fragrant forests. On one part of the route, our horses face a natural flight of rock stairs that I challenge even the nimblest pony to tackle without difficulty. We also climb perhaps the hardest hill they have done in weeks, only to find that we have gone the wrong way and have to come back down. Nevertheless, everyone manages and I realise that riding Gwen is no longer what I imagine manoeuvring a jumbo jet must be like. As we open a gate I ask for and receive, a passable [14]turn on the forehand, using only my legs and weight, which is an incredible achievement in view of Gwen's physique and history. Our lives are also made much easier now that all the horses have realised rivers are places from which to drink.

We stay in Ostabat, which to my mind is the prettiest village we have seen so far, and I announce that 'When I'm rich and famous I will buy …' Paul nods tolerantly, whilst also reminding me that not even JK Rowling could afford all the places I currently hold on my list. The equine accommodation is the best yet, an apple orchard where the *gîte* owner's daughter usually has her own pony.

Ray meets us in Ostabat, after a long and very tiring drive with the trailer from our home in the north of France, and we break the news to him that he has to sleep in a dormitory with three other people.

'But I haven't got any pyjamas,' he looks over to a woman who is checking in as we speak.

'Don't worry, she probably won't have either.'

We do our best to help him forget the night ahead by pushing litres of wine his way. In the morning he looks wan and weak.

'What's up?'

'She snored.'

'Welcome to pilgrim land.'

Then it is time for Paul and I to say goodbye to Lucy and we tell each other that we are not going to cry, though of course we do. As I dribble into my tissue, I hand over my Spanish hat and we all lose control. Then we hug for the last time and turn our attention to Okapi, who walks into the trailer with only a minor protest because he is leaving his girls.

LUCY

Arriving in the south of France, I realized what a huge undertaking this really was. The heat increased the further we went, the countryside became drier, rockier and generally dustier. Reds, oranges and yellows, the old clichés, but no less impressive for that. The long evening faded into coolness and the night was finally visible with the stars that I would get to know much better within the next two weeks. Then I settled down to considering what I was letting myself in for. Could I really do this? Thirty kilometres a day? In this heat? Was I mad? Probably. It must genetic.

The next morning, we rose early like the masochistic pilgrims we are, and set off before the heat started. The first day was gorgeous with very little road and chalk paths stretching away into nowhere. The next day was filled with leafy avenues and bubbly tarmac and straw fields, followed by more tarmac, more trees, more bubbly tarmac, more stones and more gravel. Three days later, Paul told me that we had just left Quercy and its 'ocean of stones' and that it would get easier from thereon. I haven't forgiven him yet.

On the third day, I rode for ten kilometres. The heat was oppressive and my feet were really hurting. I was wearing my trainers, which I later swapped for Paul's sandals and SOCKS (the shame)!! Riding was a very different experience from walking, and the first time was one of the easiest days, though I admit to having buttock-burn after only a few hours, so I hate to think what the others must be suffering. We were lucky with the terrain and only had to get off twice to pass very narrow bridges, but in the town it took almost an hour of toil with lorries and cars shooting past. The horses were very good, although it wasn't very well signposted and we managed to get lost twice in a place you could spit across.

Days followed days and *gîte*s followed *gîte*s, the occasional campsite added to the holiday feel. I loved every minute of it. We met lots of different people, stayed in lots of different places, each with their own stories and their own memories. Certain places and people stand out, in particular the village and villagers of St. Antoine, where we didn't hear one angry word, one complaint or grouch, although there was every reason for them to get miffed. When we left next morning, the old women kept apologising again and again for all the trouble that OUR horses had caused.

A few days later we met up with Irene. I won't say much about the place, because it was one of the most boring towns we were unfortunate enough to stay at. I walked with Irene the following day, then the day after that and the day after that. It was great fun. We philosophised and complained, exploded in idealistic joy at everything we agreed upon and viciously attacked many a stereotype (blondes, thin people, make up etc.) and American politics (George Bush). We got on very well and got drunk together on the last night in a most unpilgrimlike way. Staggering home after a very long game of pool (I lost), happy and aching still from the days walk, we went our separate ways to bed, her to her beloved tent in the horse's field, me to my little bed in our room. Now I have left her to attack the Pyrenees in the company of two young men from Belgium, and I think she's in good hands.

So I have come to the end of my holiday and of this incredible experience. I hope that you have found my brief account full of the positive vibes that I intended to convey. This trip has been unforgettable and all I want to do now is .... do it again.

And Onwards

After letting Okapi go, our first challenge is to adjust to the weight of the rucksacks on our backs. Not that we are carrying a great deal if compared with the weight usually carried by walkers, but it is enough to temporarily throw us off balance. Surprisingly the horses don't seem to notice any difference and Gwen attacks the hills in her usual fashion.

Today we are skimming the tops of valleys and getting as close to a bird's eye view as humans can without flying. I find it hard to believe that we are here with our horses. The preceding weeks seeming too unreal and the future simply unknown. Is this a version of Paul's vertigo?

Riding without Okapi is undoubtedly easier, particularly because we are now facing some very steep climbs that he would have found difficult to tackle at Gwen's preferred speed. Still, even as I acknowledge this, I can't help missing him and realising, in retrospect, how amazingly he has behaved for a freshly broken four-year-old. In spite of trying to reduce the workload and always restrict our distances to what I thought a young horse could cope with, I know that we have at times pushed him too hard. He has faced challenges that the most experienced horses would balk at: rickety bridges, impossibly narrow places for his packs, rock faces, chaotic traffic, crowds of people with cameras and so on and so on. Throughout all of this, his only resistance was an occasional refusal to be lead and the solution was simple. I tell myself and Paul that this winter I will work with him a little more and in spring look for the new owner who deserves him, but there is a catch in my voice as I speak.

The major challenge and excitement of the day is when we go through St. Jean Pied de Port, the capital of Basse Navarre and the gateway to Spain. This bustling mayhem of a town is wedged into a circle of hills at the foot of the Roncevaux pass, and its name reflects its position: at the foot of the port (Pyrenean word for pass). In the Middle Ages it was a major stopping off and converging point for pilgrims coming from Paris, Vezelay and Le Puy. Today, it is hard to imagine how they all fitted in. St. Jean Pied de Port is basically made up of one cobbled main street, rue de la Citadelle, oozing out of a ridiculously narrow valley. This is where we have to take our horses.

The girls behave impeccably, tip-toeing their way through the milling masses, though Gwen's nose is always within an inch of someone's ice-cream. At one point, where no other alternative can be found, Lubie entertains the crowds by drinking out of a bowl set aside for dogs. Then, less positively, she deposits a large mound outside a shop, which is not amusing as far as the owner is concerned. He complains and we leg it because we don't have a pooper scooper to hand. This is and always will be one of our greatest problems when riding through towns. As we meander through the throng of pilgrim photographers, all demanding that we stand and pose on their behalf, we hear someone shouting at us from a restaurant. It is Irene and her Belgian boys. We have managed to meet up again and I can let Lucy know that the trio is safe and well.

In the evening we stop at Hon, the last *gîte* before Spain, halfway up a mountain and already too high as far as I am concerned. How much higher can you go? The girls are given a huge field with incredible views, but in their view the grass is even better. I notice that we are at last getting into the pilgrim rhythm and while we do our washing and sort our kit, an Italian woman asks us how we manage to 'survive' on the *Chemin*, so I suppose we must look like pilgrim pros in comparison to the droves of freshers that have come out of St. Jean Pied de Port.

HEALTH AND PERFORMANCE REVIEW:

I have never had them before, but recognise the symptoms from the gruesome details related to me by my friends when they were pregnant. I now also connect this with questions from a seasoned cyclist about the effect of riding on our backsides, and put two and two together to come up with the horrible truth - Piles. I say nothing to Paul, and shamefacedly buy some cream in the pharmacy and find that haemorrhoid seems to be an international term. I also purchase a different potion that I hope will help to heal what I suppose must be the equivalent of bed sores on my arse where my cheek bones have worn through the skin.

He who ascends believes that he can touch the sky with his own hand.

Aimery Picaud

We start out in a heavy mist, trooping behind a long caterpillar of pilgrims making the ascent, and seeing little else. The climb is very steep and we rest frequently, but the girls cope surprisingly well, apart from a brief episode of mild hysteria when we walk past a small herd of wild ponies that show absolutely no interest at all. Then we come to the first of many flocks of sheep, their stripey gobstopper eyes staring at us with ruminant disinterest. 'Tourists, you just can't get away from them.'

As the mist lifts, the vast ranges come into view all around us; rolling expanses of varying shades and some very spiky peaks in the distance. I still find it hard to believe that we have ridden our horses up this high. As we stop to take a closer look at some other horses in a field, an English voice asks if she can take our photo and I answer in French, because I am so surprised. Once my brain has unfrazzled we manage to conduct a sensible conversation and I find out that Julia comes from Ellesmere in Shropshire, a town that is only a few miles from where I spent my childhood. She tells us that we are also the first English people she has met and she is going to Santiago too. Amazing coincidences.

After that, more climbing; more familiar faces; more new faces and all of them red and sweating. It's good to be on a horse now, but there are some people, a seventy-year old woman in particular, who grab my attention and put me to shame. She's leaping like a mountain goat and about as skinny. If I can be like that at sixty, I'll be happy. Then Vasco is sick all down Lubie's neck and continues to throw up at regular intervals until we reach the end of the today's journey. A noise that tends to draw attention. I worry inordinately, but as usual in these kinds of situations, Paul puts everything into perspective by reminding me that Vasco has eaten his own body weight in sheep dung, since starting out this morning.

Meanwhile, I try to imagine the route in the time of the real pilgrims, when the road would have been no more than a track seen dimly through the mist. Did they sing to pass the time and distance? Were they scattered or did they join together for strength and company? Without the comfort of the vast number of pilgrim hostels that exist today, they would have had to sleep where they could, and carry all of their own food. A tough call, though perhaps simpler than it would be for the current generation (by this I mean me), which cannot function without the daily shower and change of underwear. As we get near to what I presume must be the summit, we come to a mound of pilgrim debris, but it's a shrine so that's all right, I think. Actually, it just looks as if everyone has unloaded all their spare kit; hairdryers, underpants, scarves and anything else that was weighing them down. If this is getting into the pilgrim mentality you can keep it.

Then, suddenly we are in Spain, but where are the border guards? Who is going to check the veterinary certificates I so laboriously procured and copied three times over? Is this it? Just a stone block with Navarre carved out in the middle and people saying *Ola* instead of *Bonjour*? Suddenly it's all *buen Camino* and *quantos kilometros*? Everyone is speaking Spanish and I feel as if I've had my tongue cut out. How are we going to find lodgings in this new country? How are we going to buy feed for the horses? Who will we talk to? Then we walk into Roncevalles and everything falls into place.

Babette Gallard

SPANISH SECTION (EL CAMINO FRANCES):

RONCEVALLES TO SANTIAGO DE COMPOSTELA

We are in the Spanish region of Navarre, an ancient land where the traces of its past border conflicts are still very evident. Romans, Christians, Muslims and Jews have all made their mark on its architecture, as have the more graffiti inclined pilgrims of today. We are still riding on what is generically known as the St. James Way, but nothing is the same. The little red and white marker stripes have turned into yellow arrows, and the more common name for this Spanish section is the *Camino Francés*, because most of the pilgrims originally came from north of the Pyrenees.

We ride down into Roncesvalles, a settlement which consists of little more than the vast Refuge la Collegiale and a couple of restaurants devoted to the pilgrim trade. Our Lady of Roncesvalles was established in 1132, on the demand of Alfonso VI, and, thanks to the financial backing from a community of Augustinian canons, it was able to provide the charitable welcome to passing pilgrims that still exists today. To find out why they wanted to come here first place, you have to go back to 778 when Charlemagne's nephew Roland was killed and, in the tradition of the time, the bits left over were buried and acquired a holy aura. In Roland's chapel, today called Holy Spirit, pilgrims went to see the rock on which their hero tried to break his sword so that it would not fall into the hands of the Saracens, and to pray over the remains of his companions buried there.

In the 17th century, the hospital was serving over twenty thousand meals to the pilgrims each year, a trade that has been more or less taken over by the restaurants today, and with undoubtedly more profit. Putting all the cynicism aside for a moment, Our Lady of Roncesvalles is an awe-inspiring complex of chapels and cloisters, set in a saucer of woodland and cliffs. Basque mountaineers say that on occasion the ghostly echoes of Roland's final horn blow can be heard again, but today it would be thoroughly drowned out by the roar of the tourist coaches as they dump their pilgrim hoards.

Encountering the streets of London for the first time couldn't come as a greater shock to us and our horses. There are people everywhere, hordes of cyclists and walkers getting in each other's way, with our horses only adding to the confusion. Slowly and with great care, so that no one gets trodden on, we head for the first resting place in Spain for credentialed pilgrims. I like this part, because I think it means that we are given priority over all the rest, until I see people getting out of taxis and donning their rucksacks just fifty metres down the road. Fortunately, our disillusionment is short-lived and within minutes of arriving, a young Polish girl (who is doing a 3-week voluntary stint), tells us we can put the horses in the camping field that has been set aside for the overflow from the monastery. Here, the horses can roam as they want.

While I wait for Paul to complete the formalities, Gwen and Lubie are surrounded by admirers who can't get over the sight of Vasco sitting quietly by himself in Lubie's saddle. Then, a well-meaning onlooker comes over to ask if the horses like cheese. I haven't the heart to say no and take a large handful of rind that I will give Vasco later when we are alone.

With the painful preliminaries out of the way, we haul the tack off the horses and dive under the showers, which are in some portakabins next to the tents. You'd have thought the horses would want to make the most of their facilities too, lush grass and large areas of shade, but when I come out, Gwen's nose greets me at the door and I can only presume that she has been waiting. Lubie saunters over seconds later and both hang around our tent until we are forced to tether them for the sake of our neighbours.

In the evening we attend mass in the monastery chapel. An imposing building that I find lacks soul. Perhaps it is my own unhappy past in a convent school colouring my impression, but for me the whole process contrived and when the collecting dish is shoved under my nose, I finally conclude that it is no more than a performance. I leave shortly after, though it is the incense that drives me out rather than disillusionment. The smell used to make me nauseous all those years ago and still does.

Later, I speak on the phone to Lucy who tells me that the horses at home are being driven mad by the flies Okapi has brought back with him. I am amazed, because he had seemed to tolerate their relatively recent arrival under his tail, just as Gwen and Lubie had too. Our vet tells Lucy that these flies are only found in the south and horses in the north haven't developed an immunity and need to be treated straight away. Stranger still, the only solution is to use Frontline, a spray normally used on dogs and cats to get rid of fleas. Yet another lesson learned as we travel down the St. James Way.

HEALTH AND PERFORMANCE:

I have wrapped Gwen's hind heels in sticky bandage and this is working well on one though the other has a slight rub. I have decided that this is the only way because it would be impossible to shoe her every three weeks.

Vasco's paw, which had seemed to be a minor injury, is now looking very sore and we have had to bandage it too – he is sulking My bum hurts!

EQUIPMENT LOST:
Yet another bottle of shampoo

2 pairs of knickers

An inflatable cushion that I had been using on the saddle

Today we are heading towards Zubiri and finding the ride strangely harder than the Pyrenees climb, possibly because the majority is downhill on stony and uncomfortable tracks through a range of woodland that simply goes on for too long. Then we discover that Lubie has thrown a boot. We always try to check both horses regularly, but sometimes it is difficult to maintain attention. We turn round and on the way are told by a cyclist that he has seen a boot about a kilometre back. We eventually find it with the help of a number of other walkers – sometimes it helps to be so conspicuous.

Now that we are in Spain, one of the differences we notice most is the number of cyclists. Hordes of them, which can sometimes be difficult to deal with on the narrow tracks, though on the whole everyone is very polite and bellowing *Buen Camino-o-o-o* as they whip past seems to be part of the two-wheeled etiquette. I bellow 'igualmente,' in return, but suspect they never hear me.

Far more unpleasant, is the dreadful amount of rubbish we see all along the route and close to it. This is a real disappointment and obviously a problem the authorities are trying to tackle, because there are repeated reminders to keep the country clean. Why this is so much worse in Spain than France is hard to explain, though I remember that when I lived in Portugal the behaviour was very similar. If this is a specifically Iberian aspect of the culture, the toilet paper (and worse) lining the route certainly is not. We have seen it everywhere and wonder why it is that pilgrims, who really need to relieve themselves, also lose any sense of shame in the process. Couldn't they at least bury the traces for the sake of the people who follow on behind?

A traffic jam on the *Camino* is a situation we have never encountered or anticipated before, but when we get to Zubiri, an unattractive sprawl of houses along a main route, our worst fears are confirmed. In spite of seeing at least ten hostels and small hotels, everywhere is full and to make things really difficult, it is a fiesta day too. This means that because of the possibility of drunken behaviour the sports hall, which people are usually allowed to sleep in, is closed. Brilliant timing on our part.

The good bit is that in spite of my gloom and grumpiness, Paul manages to negotiate a field for the horses – in Spanish! I am impressed and my spirits lift, marginally, until I realise that this will also be our bedroom and we don't have a tent any more. We sneak an illegal shower in an overflowing[15] refugio and then visit the fiesta with the intention of drinking enough to ensure we fall asleep, no matter how uncomfortably. As we make our way down we see Julia walking in and bellow over the busy road that everywhere is full.

'No problem,' she smiles back brightly. 'I've booked'

So where are your angels now, when we need them, Philippe?

Actually we quite enjoy ourselves. A Spanish group is playing in the square and dancers of all ages quickly fill it. We notice that everyone is able to dance in the traditional style, without a trace of Anglo or American music being allowed to slip in. The Spanish certainly know how to party, starting late and finishing early without taking any breaks in the middle. We survive until eleven o'clock and then stagger back for our noisy night under the stars.

FEEDING SPANISH STYLE

Six o'clock in the morning and I assume that I must have slept, because I am waking up and only remember some of the pain. Anyway, when we finally emerge, we look a great deal better than the revellers who are still drinking on the street outside. The bad news is that Gwen is lame and a closer look shows that the bandage I have put on to protect her heel has slipped up and cut into her [16]pastern. I curse myself for not bothering to take it off the night before. What now? Find a farrier? Panic? I cut the bandage off and see that it is not deep in spite of Gwen's obvious pain, so perhaps she is just a bit of a drama queen. I use some of our magic antiseptic spray and decide to take her into the river to see if cold water and then exercise will take the swelling down. Half an hour later my prayers are answered. She has recovered completely and there are no visible ill-effects. I've got away with it this time. I know I won't get another chance.

After this difficult start we enjoy the ride, in spite of the heat and some difficult sections involving long flights of steep steps, nothing fazes our girls now. We stop off for a coffee in a village on the way, with Gwen, Lubie and Vasco drawing the usual fan club, except that this time we are in a hurry so we push on so that we can get to the refuge long before opening time in order to ensure a space - no sleeping outside tonight. While we wait at the door of the convent of Santa Trinidad, Paul starts talking to some Italians who tell him there is another arm of the St. James

Way that goes down to Rome. Oh-oh. I have a feeling I know where this is leading.

We sleep in an annexe next to the church, and the horses are tethered in a small garden at the back where the grass is non-existent. We have to start looking for food in Spain and as the Spanish speaker (two years in school, forty years ago), Paul volunteers to go. He is gone for over three hours and has a story to tell when he gets back. The poor man has been everywhere, on foot mainly and latterly in a taxi, but everyone, however well meant, directs him to the wrong place. Finally, it is the taxi driver who takes pity and calls a friend.

I wouldn't normally include matadors on my list of acquaintances, never mind friends, but in this instance I would have kissed the man if I had been there, and not just because he has been kind. Paul is taken to a vast estate where horses are bred and trained for the bull fights. Impressive, by all accounts, and the owner every woman's dream. A muscled hunk Paul is glad that neither Lucy nor I are there to see. Anyway, the hunk shows Paul what he feeds his horses and offers to give him some, no charge.

When Paul proudly shows me the large sack full of whole oats, I don't know what to say. Yes, whole oats are fed to horses, I have done so myself in Germany and Portugal, but only because the horses were familiar with it. In my world, oats are crushed and measured carefully according to the type of horse and levels of work. Our horses have only ever had limited amounts and never whole. I consider the choices.

Don't give them the oats and they go hungry.

Feed the oats and deal with the risk of colic.

As I ponder, Gwen's nose is already elongating like a snake in the direction of the sack and Lubie is fixing it with her Houdini gaze. So what else can I do? I feed small amounts and watch them carefully?

During the night I get up five times and each time find them dozing peacefully amongst large piles of healthy muesli poo. Another lesson learnt on the *Camino*.

HEALTH AND PERFORMANCE:

Gwen's heels are worrying, but I cannot see that finding a farrier at this stage is a viable alternative. I have to find a way of using the bandages without any side effects.

The bite on Gwen's back seems to be under control. I am protecting it as much as I can.

Lubie developing a pressure sore - we are protecting it.

Vasco has a worrying lump on his stomach though it does not seem to hurt him. We may have to visit a vet if it doesn't get better. His claw needs some attention too.

Backside is painful once again, because our second inflatable cushion has a puncture

DRAWBRIDGES AND DRAWBACKS

Little information is available about the routes followed by pilgrims in the 11th century, once they had crossed the Pyrenees. In fact, it looks as if there was a good deal of to-ing and fro-ing until Alfonso VI, King of Castile, and Sancho Ramirez, King of Aragon, started to sort it all out. Both of them got rid of the river and road tolls and encouraged the foundation of hospitals in major sites in their regions, so that by the 12th century the infrastructure of the *Camino* Francés had been created. Pamplona was the starting point for the established itinerary that went through Puente la Reina, Estella, Logrono, Najera and Burgos.

Pamplona was made famous by Ernest Hemingway, and he was duly rewarded for the freebie publicity by having a street named after him, Avenida de Hemingway, but Paul and I don't like bull fighting, even though we do like his books. We're only interested in Pamplona's history.

Like most of Spain's cities, just about everyone has been here at some time or other. In the winter of 74-75 B.C. the area served as a camp for the Roman general Pompey. He is thought to be the founder of "Pompaelo" (Pamplona) and the man behind the great steam baths, which had unfortunately gone by the time pilgrims were ready to make use of them. By 409, Pamplona was controlled by the Visigoths and from the eighth century it was dominated by the Moors. By the 10th century, everything had begun to settle down and Pamplona was ready to benefit from the new fashion of going on pilgrimages to Santiago de Compostela, which is where the real development of culture and commerce started. During the 18th century, several beautiful palaces were built, such as the Casa Consistorial or Town Hall and the neoclassic facade of the Cathedral was undertaken in 1783. Today Pamplona is said to have the highest quality of life in Spain, though this is a little harder to see.

As we ride into Pamplona, we are aware of all the must-be-seen parts, but this is the first really big city our horses have encountered and how they or we will react is anybody's guess. First, there is the drawbridge into the citadel. I hold my breath and coax Gwen nervously while Paul holds the camera. Perhaps she senses that something is expected and decides to disappoint us. We'll never know, but my look of utter disbelief when she walks over without hesitation makes a good picture anyway.

Next, we have the tiny cobbled streets to tackle, inevitably one-way, the wrong way, and full of cars. Our horses take it all in their stride and when we reach an empty fountain a group of builders refill it for us from their buckets. This is all just too good to be true. Then photos, photos, photos and more people and more cars as we follow the Bull Run, our horses behaving as if this is just every day stuff while we are behaving like first-timers. What a beautiful city. What a shame we can't park our transport and take the time to see more, but now we have to negotiate the far less pleasant suburbs and their incessant roundabouts. I nearly run into the back of Paul when he suddenly stops halfway round.

'Look at that!'

I look in the direction of his frantically gesticulating finger to see a pilgrim hauling his rucksack out of a taxi and preparing to walk back up the trail. Then we end up in Cizur Menor where we have to find somewhere for us and our horses to stay.

The first [17]*albergue* seems pleasant from the outside, but the owner is less welcoming. She tells us that she won't take horses anymore because their owners never clean up the mess they leave behind.

A spectre of guilt shudders uncomfortably down my spine and I don't argue.

The second *albergue* is in what used to be the local chapel and is now run by the order of the Maltese Cross. Here, the volunteers, two young Polish girls, do everything they can to find facilities for horses, though in reality they are non-existent. Finally, they manage to speak to the owner of the corn field behind the chapel, who agrees to the horses being tethered there. There is no grass and everything is as dry as a dustbowl. Our horses deserve better after a hard day's work and we search hopelessly for anything vaguely green and edible in the nearby verges and scrappy patches of land, but it is all unappetising and valueless scrub.

Next, we have to go to the Decathlon sports store to replace some of our equipment and buy the small bags of high-value horse feed we have seen on sale in the French stores. Gwen needs this and we can carry it easily. We find a taxi and pay the distance, only to find that horses do not feature in this area. The equestrian products are crowded into a small corner and provide nothing we need. Failure, almost, except that we are able to buy a compact tent to replace our ten-second wonder which we had returned with Okapi, because it was too big to carry on our backs.

When we get back to Cizur Menor we go to the horses and immediately see that something is wrong. The bag holding our tools and veterinary store is empty, its contents scattered across the ground and our most important and expensive tool gone. Next, we notice that Gwen has a boot on, crooked and on the wrong hoof. This is worrying, but what can we do? Before we left, I had noticed three teenage boys in the porch of the chapel and near to the horses. At the time it hadn't crossed my mind that they would do anything to our horses or equipment, now I am not so sure. I go to the volunteers and warn them that there may be someone around who is not a true pilgrim. They offer to call the police, but there is no point, so we just check the rest of our bags and hide our most valuable items.

Later, just before we prepare for bed, I look for the mobile phone to make my customary call to Lucy. Gone. I have encountered problems with petty theft in Spain before though, naively, I had not expected it to be here on the *Camino*. Now we discuss in all seriousness calling the police, but first Paul suggests we try calling our own phone to see if it rings anywhere in the dormitory where we are staying. Enough said. It is found, but our trust is broken and I find it hard to speak to anyone there in the morning. We agree that to call the police would only be counter-productive, because of the fuss it would cause and possible retaliation from the guilty party or his/her friends.

Today, we get out at seven o'clock, because we can't wait to leave and the early start is good. Rain is in the air, which can be unpleasant, though at the moment anything is preferable to the intense heat we have been warned about as we cross the plains to Burgos. The horses seem to attract harbingers of doom. Our last dismal-dirger was a Frenchman staying in the *gîte* d'etape at the foot of the Pyrenees. He wasn't walking, but claimed a right to tell everyone else what to do because his brother was. 'Horses from the north won't make it in the heat. I've read about some pilgrims who … the forecast is for plus forty … if you don't take salt you'll …. blah …'

At the time, I smiled and pointed to the grey sky with a knowing shamanist look I hoped would be convincing. And if that didn't work, the next look that said *I'm not listening* was very clear. Even so, now I am worrying. Every centimetre of the landscape ahead is defined by the lines of fields ploughed and put down to crops – the archetypical Spanish plain I remember from school photographs, where I know the rain doesn't fall, though today it looks as if it might be about to. Please, if there is a god, please, please, please.

'Pray, look better, sir,' quoth Sancho; 'those things yonder are no giants, but windmills, and the arms you fancy, are their sails, which being whirled about by the wind, make the mill go.'

'It is a sign,' cried Don Quixote, 'thou art but little acquainted with adventures.'

In between slogging over a yellow billiard board, we encounter some very steep climbs with a few difficult descents. One particular ascent takes us directly under a long line of windmills and bang on cue the wind picks up. We have seen a number of wind farms already, though only from a distance. Now we are walking underneath them and they are working overtime. The noise is not unpleasant, though it is loud and I brace myself for Gwen's reaction. Her back is tense and her ears are rotating like radar dishes on Ecstasy. I wait for the explosion, but instead she just gives me one of her sighs and plods on.

On the summit of the Sierra del Perdon, a fantastic pinnacle that gives us a view over what seems like the whole of Spain, we are greeted by a massive sculpture of a group of larger than life pilgrims with their horses and donkeys. Of course, I have to pose in front of them for a photo, though with the wind being so strong it is difficult to stand still, so the torture is mercifully brief.

Our only disappointment of the day is when we find that the churches and cemeteries really are all locked, as the guidebooks had told us they would be. At about midday, we pass through Puente la Reina, a very pretty town with a strong sense of history reinforced by the remains of walls and several religious buildings. The 12th century church with its Romanesque and star-shaped ogival vaults demands more attention and we allow ourselves a half-hour break, but then we have to get back on the trail. Later, we meet Irene again and walk with her into Villatuerta where we tether the girls to trees at the edge of a park – it's far from ideal, although it is the best grass they have had in days. Nevertheless, I am becoming increasingly fretful, and no doubt irritating, about the need to find feed, so Paul goes out to speak to the locals again, proving that it is truly amazing what you can do with just twenty words and a lot of gestures. An hour later, he comes back with the news that he has managed to track someone down who has recommended a man called Pablo, in Estella. We must go there tomorrow and see what he can do for us.

Villatuerta is a very small town and if there is anything notable to see here we miss it. Still, our evening in the *albergue* is pleasant enough, because tonight's pilgrims don't feel the need to massage each other in the passage or pop their blisters at the table. The owner is obviously fazed by having someone with horses stay there, but he seems prepared to give it a go, even when we fill his narrow hallway with our stinking tack and Lubie dumps a huge pile of muesli poo in front of his doorway. The owner is so unfazed that I wonder if he's on something he'd like to share, then we meet his wife who definitely isn't. She banishes our horses to a piece of scrub at the other end of the park, and points a finger at the back yard where we are to put our tack. It was a nice while it lasted.

Over dinner we meet an Australian couple, Robert and Moya, and find that we are sharing our cupboard-sized dormitory with them. As we coyly change for dinner (clean t-shirt in my case), I check him over for the tight nylon underpants and big belly that Paul has decided are the trademarks of a snorer/farter. He passes the test and I look forward to a peaceful night, though perhaps I snore without knowing it. Robert and Moya have been walking for some weeks already, and seem far more seasoned travellers than us in every respect. I warm to them quickly, as I do to a South African man and woman, Mani and Amanda, who will be writing about their experiences for a number of magazines when they get back home. What they will say about us?

The only negative aspect of our stay here is that Vasco will definitely have to stay outside for the night. Up until this point we have managed to dodge the Spanish dislike of dogs by smuggling him in when people are not looking, but here it is clear that the proprietor's wife is in charge and on the lookout for delinquent pilgrims. Vasco goes out in the garden and curls up miserably on my jacket, while I lie awake half the night waiting for the howls to start. They don't, and it's another lesson learnt for me. The boy knows the score. He might not like it, but he knows when there is no alternative.

HEALTH AND PERFORMANCE REVIEW:

New saddle cushion bought in Decathlon now a great relief for my backside.

Paul's knee causing problems towards the end of the day.

Vasco's stomach lump has burst and seems to be improving as a result – a relief.

Lubie is developing a gall under her saddle and the hair around it is going grey – we have to watch this carefully.

Gwen's heels holding out well with the bandages, and the last remaining hornet lump on her back is showing signs of swelling again.

Saints and Angels

Estella, where bread is good, the wine excellent, meat and fish are abundant and which is full of delicacies.
Aimery Picaud

We start out with the intention of doing a short day, because Gwen's back is worrying and both horses are showing signs of being tired, but first we must stop off in Estella to find Pablo and hopefully some oats. The directions are imprecise, though experience has taught me that Paul will reach his goal, no matter how high the odds are stacked against him.

We ride up to a church on the edge of the town, and I let the horses graze while he searches for a house that is supposed to be nearby. Five minutes later he is back, a broad grin all over his face. 'You've got to come and see this.' He points to a large door covered in horse shoes and a variety of other decorations on the equine theme. Then, through a small grill, we see a stable yard piled high with the tack and equipment used by picadors. So, whoever Pablo is, we are in no doubt that he loves horses and either was or still is strongly connected with **los toreros**.

A fleeting moral dilemma makes me pause for all of a nanosecond. I detest bullfights, but in terms of what we are looking for - food for our horses - the chances are definitely improving. Our spirits lift, though only briefly because after another five minutes and a great deal of knocking on wood, Paul has only been able to raise someone we presume to be either Pablo's wife or mother.

An elderly lady crosses the yard, in slippers, slowly. This does not look hopeful. I try to smile as she hands a plastic bag to Paul before he has even begun to embark on his explanation of who we are and why we are here.

'Go to Santiago for me,' she tells him, while curtly waving her hand in a refusal of payment.

Paul and I draw breath to protest, but she has already shut the door in our faces and we can only accept her generosity as yet another reminder that walking the *Camino* is a great deal more than just another hike. We feed the horses immediately, whole oats again, and this time I am less nervous, because they have survived the first lot without any obvious problems.

Estella is another of King Sancho Ramirez's pilgrim initiatives, the first stone being laid at the foot of Lizarra Castle, on the right bank of the Ega, in 1090, but its name comes from a legend that shepherds, alerted by a miraculous shower of stars (estrella - star), discovered the statue called Our Lady of Le Puy. Who knows what they saw and why. All we can say with any certainty is that Our Lady's presence brought the pilgrims in their thousands from the north, some of them lepers looking for help in the Saint Lazarus hospital, and others stopping to enjoy the buoyant economy. By the 14th Century the size of the Frankish population was such that Provencal was still being spoken there. Today, although these traces have almost entirely disappeared, the pilgrims keep coming and the churches like San Pedro de la Rua are still doing a good trade.

With oats inside our girls the ride goes well and we cover a good distance before the sun has risen high enough to shrivel us. Then we come to something that not many pilgrims, however zealous, can pass by without a pause. A fountain of wine, free and gushing from a tap in the wall. It's those angels again. As we draw to a halt we see Irene sitting at its base with a contented smile on her face, already two glasses gone.

How the [18]Bodegas de Irache manages to cover the cost of thousands of thirsty pilgrims like us drinking its produce I don't know, and after three glasses don't care, even at ten o'clock in the morning. We drink one more each, share a bar of chocolate and then get back on the route before we lose complete control of our faculties and resolve.

Another 10 kilometres further on and the sun begins to take its toll. Everyone in the team is tired so we take a break in Villamayor de Monjardin, a small, picturesque village with perhaps one of the most attractively finished *albergue*s we have come across. Our instinct is to stay here, but there is nowhere suitable for the horses, so we just allow ourselves a break and a cold beer before moving on. Nevertheless, the short half hour is an interesting one because we start talking to Rachel, a Dutch girl, who is working as a volunteer for the Christian Group running the *albergue*. Books proclaiming The Word are on the table and I feel my hackles rise. In fact, we find ourselves to be broadly in agreement on a number of issues and only differ on the means of achieving our goals.

In spite of our esoteric talk, the need to feed our horses dominates everything else. The small bag of oats is almost all gone and now we must find some more. As we approach Los Arcos, with Irene walking beside us, I can think of little to say and worry even more because Gwen is clearly either very tired or uncomfortable for a reason that I can't yet define. Then one of those St. James Way angels turns up again, in heavy disguise.

John lives in a large, three bedrooms with en suite, camper van. Its white exterior standing out incongruously against the dusty backdrop of the landscape where he parks, but his motives are one hundred percent *Camino*. As he tops up our water bottles, he explains that after completing the journey himself years before, he retired and left London to do what he is still doing now some five years on, driving up and down the *Camino*, offering food, water, a variety of palliative care for aching muscles and, most importantly from our point of view, local information.

'What do you need to know?'

Anywhere else it would have seemed a strange kind of question, but here it is spot-on.

'We need to find feed.' I splutter through my third biscuit.

'No problem, there is an agricultural co-operative in Los Arcos, just take the first left and then when you see ....' This is when I go into neutral and assume Paul is listening, only catching up for the last bit when I am sure it doesn't involve directions. 'Show them your horses and tell them that you are pilgrims and you'll most likely get it free of charge.'

'What do we ask for?'

'*Cebada* or *aven*a, your horses will eat both.'

Our horses are so hungry they would eat ground up pilgrim blisters by this point, but John is right, down to the very last detail, and we dub him St. John.

At the co-operative we are able to fill our collapsible bucket brim-full with oats, and then a man calls us over and indicates that we should follow him. We do so and stare in total amazement as he takes out a sack and goes to what must be his own warehouse to give us oats that are clearly of a much higher quality.

Next, we have to find somewhere to stay and make our way through the narrow streets with a large sack of oats balanced precariously on Lubie's back while Paul walks. It falls off every second step and we are both thoroughly pissed off by the time we reach the refuge, only to be told that it is full. We are directed to another and find space for ourselves, but only a vast expanse of burnt grass with no trees for the horses. I feel terrible. This is not what they deserve after yet another hard day. Then I take Gwen's saddle off. The hornet sting that had been clearing up so well has now grown to the size of a camel's hump. My poor, poor Gwen.

ON FOOT - IN ESPADRILLES

Her pendulous underlip was trembling as if she were about to cry.

From These Are My People, by Alan Marshall

Yesterday I was concerned, today I know that Gwen is in big trouble. The bite wound has opened up again and the lymph gland under her elbow is swollen. I curse myself for not finding time to get a course of antibiotics from the vet before we left - the most basic precautionary measure. Now we, and more unjustly Gwen, have to learn our lesson the hard way. We have to find a vet and a place to rest up. We load Lubie with all of the saddle bags and leave Gwen to carry only the saddle with a very loose girth. Our aim is to walk to Torres del Rio where John has told us there is a horse farm. Our hope is that here we will meet someone who can help us to find a vet and perhaps sell us some more oats. We have also seen that for only the second time since coming into Spain, this *albergue* is listed as one that takes horses. Surely one of these options will be helpful.

The 8 kilometre walk is relatively easy, though I am only wearing a pair of very tattered espadrilles, with socks, which is all I have other than my riding boots. I must look very odd. As we progress, people who have seen us before ask what is wrong and when we tell them everyone is concerned and very sympathetic.

In Torres del Rio, a relatively small village, we slog our weary way up to Mari's *albergue,* which is of course at the very top of a hill. An old woman greets us and Paul quickly finds out that willingness to take horses does not extend to providing accommodation for them. She wants us to rig up an electric fence in the wheat field at the back of the house, which makes me think that the other riders who have been here before must have had some form of back-up. When we say that we can't, she indicates a small square of land that has been roughly fenced off and clearly used by horses at some point in the distant past. This will do fine, except that we are surrounded by acres of the most beautiful, blossoming almond trees and Lubie has already spotted them. The fence had better be good.

Next, we try to ask her about vets, places to buy feed and the horse farm. Her answer to every question is a strong negative and my heart sinks lower than ever before. Meanwhile, my poor Gwen is suffering visibly; she is reluctant to walk and is grunting uncomfortably. How could I have been so stupid? How could I have ever considered subjecting our horses to travelling 1600 kilometres over difficult terrain and in these conditions? As we walk back to the *albergue* to arrange rooms for ourselves, I am close to tears and would have suggested calling the whole thing off, if Mari and her husband hadn't arrived to save the day. More angels, this time in shell suits.

In desperation I ask them once again if there is a vet nearby and am told there is not, but they will try calling one in from Logrono. Now I feel faint with relief and finally have to sit down when they tell me that a horse specialist will be arriving sometime later in the afternoon. I thank God, or whoever it is who arranges these things, and then set off with Paul to lug gallons of water up the steep slope to where our precious horses are so patiently waiting in the tinder dry field. They whinny as we approach and I wonder why they are so tolerant and infinitely forgiving. In their place I would have kicked me into the middle of next week.

Seven hornet stings to kill a horse, three an adult and two a child – the old saying echoes round my head like a bad tune, even though I know it's not true. When the vet finally arrives his face says it all.

'No riding for at least three weeks, may be more.'

He doesn't really need to tell me because deep down I already know. He gives Gwen an antibiotic shot and tells me that I must administer the rest of the five-day course myself. I feel foolish and guilty. How many other horses does he have to deal with that have been pushed too hard on the *Camino*?

While he is there we take the opportunity to show him Lubie's pressure sore and he confirms that we just have to keep it clean and covered, so at least my diagnosis was right here, and I suppose that after nearly one thousand kilometres this is not bad going. Without the hornets, we would only have Gwen's scuffed heels and Vasco's intermittently sore paw to report, minor injuries well within our capabilities of treating. In fact, with our bandaging, both horse and dog are looking better than they have for a long time.

Now we are proposing a five-day stay to ensure that the antibiotics have time to take effect and the healing process is well underway before we get back on the road, but on foot, until Gwen is fully recovered.

New groups of pilgrims are coming into our path, and I have to accept that we will reach Santiago later than Irene and the others who we have overtaken in the past, an observation that leads me to consider again the wisdom of riding with horses at all. I look at Gwen grazing contentedly now that the vet has gone. What would she or Lubie do if given the choice? I try to anthropomorphise our beloved pair to imagine their thoughts – a fairly ridiculous exercise considering our individual starting points, but if Disney can do it then so can I.

First there is Lubie, a fairly typical race horse. Initially unaffectionate and blandly compliant. She was too slow, and the hard fact is that animals bred for the track are only kept for their performance. Under-performance is dealt with in one of two ways, recycling as dog meat or sale to people like us. In the five months that we have owned her, Lubie has become a vocal and affectionate friend who has clearly made it her mission to protect Paul, the learner human, on her back. While riding behind the two of them I have seen examples of wilful equine disobedience with the best intentions; Lubie insisting on pulling over to the right in spite of Paul's efforts to steer her left, because of course she could see the loose soil where he could not. Or, the other times when she has soothed him past rumbling tractors where one would expect it to be the other way round. In human form, I see Lubie as the ageing repertory actress, fag in hand and skirt too short, but heart as soft as putty where *her boy* is concerned.

'Don't worry darling, I've seen it all before.'

Surely this and her persistent bellows of greeting can be taken as some sign of affection and appreciation of the life we have brought her into.

And what about my Gwen? From what I understand, her relationship with humans got off to a bad start, and continues to be based on a very brittle layer of trust. As far as I know, the story is that a fairly hefty and rough rider tried to break her, with very little success. Her habit of standing stock still as a precursor to launching herself into the air and, I guess from the state of her spine, throwing herself to the ground, may have been developed as a result of some serious misunderstandings. Whatever the history, the outcome was abandonment in a field, cared for minimally by a kind, but cash-strapped man who did the only thing he could, allow her to live. As a result, Gwen is a feisty character, looking for points to score against a world that has treated her badly, though she is also utterly loyal if persuaded. Spoken to in the right way, and at the right time, there is nothing she will not do for me. Her habit of stopping to turn her head and heave a thunderous sigh before tackling steep slopes would eliminate her from any kind of competitive riding, but who cares? I have the time to wait and see no point in initiating a fight. Anyway, I know how she feels. On this tenuous and somewhat ludicrous basis, Gwen and I are invincible. She will tackle any hill, any obstacle and any other challenge I set her. Her only major disobedience, her insistence (in spite of everything I try to do) on walking two centimetres behind me when I am on the ground, which invariably ends up in shredded heels, mine. If this is her own, very special way of expressing affection, then it's fine by me. I'll just wear bigger boots.

Mari and her family take us and our animals to their hearts. Sacks of bread and melons for the horses appear as if from nowhere, people I have never seen before try to tempt Vasco with all kinds of delicacies that he embarrassingly refuses, while I find myself cuddled and comforted by older women as if I were sixteen-year-old girl. When Mari has a photograph taken with the vast numbers of pilgrims who have turned up to stay, she puts herself firmly between Paul and I.

Mari's place is a magnet, defying all claims that only the *albergues* at the beginnings or ends of the stages set out in the guide books can thrive. It is packed every minute of the day, and on our first evening there an Italian couple we met only two days before, include us in a meal they are making for twenty other pilgrims. Languages battle for space over the table: Italian, Spanish, Portuguese, German and English, but everyone seems able to understand and be understood. An amazing cultural cocktail, trumped only by Joel, an Italian who speaks English with a broad Dublin accent and looks as if he has come straight off a Wanted poster.

When it is finally time for us to fall into bed, we have the usual Vasco problem. Mari and her family are still here and are showing no signs of going home, it's only next door anyway. I do not want to be seen to abuse their incredible generosity, so we put my jacket on the ground outside in the backyard and do our best to explain the situation to him. He eyes us knowingly and we slink guiltily up the stairs.

Five minutes later there is a knock on the door, it is Mari's mother-in-law, the one who had been most vocal about the no-dog rule. She winks and points to Vasco who is at her heel. 'It's too noisy down there,' she tells us. 'Too many pilgrims sleeping on the mattresses outside. The dog will be better with you.'

From here the conspiracy is a thin one, Vasco joins us every night and everyone pretends not to see.

Today Paul is walking back to Los Arcos to find a cash machine, while I treat Gwen's wound and give her the antibiotic injection. She seems much recovered and both horses are quite content in the field, though there is not a great deal to eat, but of course Mari and her husband are already one step ahead. When I go up to the field sometime later I find him strimming the long dry grass on the other side of the fence. 'For the horses,' he tells me. 'They can find some good new grass under all this.'

Later when Paul and I go to the shop to buy some lunch, the woman behind the counter points to a huge box of bread. 'Para los caballos.'

I've never been very keen on feeding large amounts of bread to horses, but then I've always been told to avoid whole oats and since been proved wrong. So I give it try and watch them carefully, because it is fiesta time in the region until Tuesday and every other shop or business is shut.

In their field the horses are not fussy and chew thoughtfully on long baguettes without a care for how comic they look, but I can't laugh, because it is all too clear that while Lubie has lost some weight she is still round and sleek, whereas Gwen on the same food looks like a case for the RSPCA. It is not all bad news, though, because Vasco, with his newly acquired understanding of the Spanish culture, is loving his independence. Now we can go into bars and leave him outside without feeling guilty because he's got the picture. Waiting for us gives him time to sniff out the talent, which this morning involves bringing four canine mates back with him, much to the amusement of Mari and family.

Later on in the day, three Spanish riders turn up in the street outside. They have ridden from Roncesvalles in three days, which is fast, and are using traditional Spanish saddles that I like the look of, except for the sharp metal stirrups that could do some real damage. The horses are ideal for the job, small, stocky and hardy, but even they are obviously feeling the strain and are streaked with old sweat.

I walk up to the testosterone group, presuming that some sort of gesture like slapping them on the shoulders and saying *Hey Hombre*, is needed, but as a female foreigner I don't even show up on their radar. They don't want to hear about me, the distance we have done or why our horses are taking a break now. So I turn feminine and listen meekly while they shout about the number of blankets that are needed under the saddle – one for every day of riding, which would mean sitting on the height of a skyscraper in our case – and what kind of ropes are best for tethering. Half of what they say in gunfire-fast Spanish might as well have been about flying to Mars, but they clearly think my glazed expression indicates that I am impressed. I'm sure it's a technique they use with their wives.

Torres del Rio teaches both of us a great deal. It teaches me about generosity without strings, about our horses: how vulnerable they are and how much they mean to me, and about my own inadequacies. Meanwhile, Paul discovers his first example of the stork anarchy that will fascinate him until the day we leave and fill a hundred megabytes of camera memory.

'It's their audacity and their design,' he tells me, while I try to persuade Gwen that waiting until Paul has finished his photograph is an important point of equine etiquette. 'The nest on the bell tower is a two finger salute to religion and authority.'

I suspect it is more a matter of finding a flat place where no one will shoot lead up their babies' bums, but I can appreciate his fascination. Just as I appreciate the strange bonging sound made by Spanish bells, five minutes past the hour. Paul explains this in terms of the metal they are made of (not bronze), a good reason maybe, though for me it still sounds like someone hitting an enamel bath with a hammer. My belief is that the bell towers are just a tourist sham and the little shed in Dona Rodrigues' back yard is the real source of the noise and bad timing.

In the evening Paul and I walk together into Los Arcos to see the bull-run that is the focal point of the fiesta, but first we stop off at an *albergue* to sort out some emails. As we wait, a man hobbles painfully into the room. A sixty-five-year-old German, with a heart condition and arthritic knees, who has cycled from Le Puy en Velay in seventeen days. I tell Paul to remind me of him if I ever complain that I am too old to do something.

The bull run is not an impressive event. The bulls aren't interested in the amusement and refuse to charge as expected, even when they are goaded with electric prods. Meanwhile, the macho and brave Rioja-powered humans run before the bulls have even arrived. Paul's claim to have been in the same town at the same time as a bull, ranks just as high in the bravado stakes, and I am deeply unimpressed. For Vasco it is a different matter. He shakes with either rage or fear, we can't decide which, and barks furiously whenever a bull threatens to come near the barrier. Perhaps he is trying to take control and admonish them in the way he does with the horses when they misbehave, but whatever his reasoning it is not popular with the rest of the audience, so we watch for ten minutes and then leave. Seeing animals goaded and taunted for the pleasure of a gawking and persistently dissatisfied crowd is simply not fun.

ES MUY BUEN

After five days Gwen is improving. The glandular swelling has gone down and so has the sting. We can consider leaving, though of course one of us will have to walk.

The figs are ripening at last and we and the horses eat a load with the predictable results. The girls also accept a courgette from an old man who is cooking a huge pan of paella in his garage, which I would not have expected to suit the equestrian palate, but then again the *Camino* has taught me that what I know about horses would fit on the back of a postcard.

We are passing through the seemingly infinite expanse of the Rioja vineyards, beautiful, picturesque and tantalisingly full of ripe grapes, but we resist the temptation to eat them because it is part of the pilgrim code, unlike dumping the contents of one's bowels, *al fresco*, which obviously isn't.

Progress is harder now that one of us is always on foot. I try walking in my boots, except that a bruised sole is making every step agony, so we stop in Logrono to buy some sandals and suddenly I feel as if I am walking on air. Outside Logrono, we are able to buy some blankets for the horses, two each, which provides ample padding and ease for my mind. Thank you macho Spanish riders. You may have not listened to one word I had to say and I may have only understood ten of yours, but if our meeting helps our horses, it was worth every frustrating second. Meanwhile, as always, I am worrying about finding feed.

Just as I begin to despair we pass a closed barn and find a huge pile of spilled oats outside. We let the horses eat their fill.

Tonight, we are staying in Navarette, at an equestrian centre that (as the proprietors Katerina and Miguel tell us) welcomes every kind of animal, including llamas. Better still, Vasco is allowed to sleep in our room. Here, we are just two more in a huge list of riders and their horses who have been on the St. James Way before us. We are shown photo after photo of every variation of traveller, some good, some impressive, some distinctly strange, but all interesting and inspiring. We read their accounts of themselves, the places they have been and the places they want to go to. It's a humbling experience and I wonder how we will compare when we write ours. There is one man who has travelled for four years with his horses and plans to go on to Istanbul. Another woman who has travelled alone and slept predominantly outside. The Austrian family who started from Vienna ... and so the list goes on. I can only ask myself where was I when they were doing this, and why has it taken me so long to get here?

In the evening we go out for a meal and find that once again we are in a town that is having its fiesta, but perhaps it is just that every town is having a fiesta every day. The bands are playing and we sit outside, in between showers of rain, to eat tapas and drink the local Rioja. The only aspect we are not so keen on is the very real bull fight we can hear in raucous progress. Later, the very minute our heads hit the pillow, the fireworks start up. Vasco growls and we worry about the girls. When we look out of the window they seem calm and happy in their enclosure. They've seen and heard it all before.

This morning we rise early and do our best to creep quietly out of the house, but Miguel is awake and just as we are about to leave he comes out to wish us well.

'Buen *Camino*.' He says with his hand on Gwen's neck. 'Es buen que hacen ustedes. Es muy buen.' The words carry more feeling than it's possible to convey in their repetition, and I can't think of a big enough reply, so I mumble a hopeless thanks and hope that the lump in my throat is obvious enough to show that I understand.

Now down to practicalities. Because of the previous night's rain, I have not been able to do any washing, which means I am having to wear the same socks for two days running. For many people this is not a big issue, while for me it is akin to stepping into dog shit with bare feet. My skin creeps at the thought, but there is no other alternative, because riding without socks is impossible. Then, as if this isn't bad enough, my nose is peeling off in little flaps of flaky white skin that I can see when I cross my eyes, and of course when you have a flap of flaky white skin on your nose, you always cross your eyes. This is when I realise that Gwen and I have a great deal in common, particularly with respect to being prone to any condition that is either unsightly or unfortunate. Her nose peels. My nose peels. I am clumsy, angular and can never be elegant no matter how hard I try. Like Gwen's mane, my hair grows in ten different versions of vertical, and like her I have a hundred scars from a variety of completely unnecessary accidents. Then, also like Gwen, I have no real interest in food. I graze impatiently and briefly, finding any kind of complicated eating like drinking soup from a spoon, a boring waste of time. So perhaps the real reason we get on has nothing to do with my legendary skills as a rider and tamer of wild beasts, just simply because we recognise our mutual inadequacies.

I think of this as we slog down the trail, passing people who are tending the vines in a very manual and individual way, which prompts me to consider the merits of mechanisation and whether it is entirely beneficial. Wine is over-produced anyway, so why produce it even faster and take out the human element that has brought people together from all over the world, just as the *Camino* does now?
Progress for progress' sake is a very one-sided business.

Further along, we find that many sections of the route follow long stretches of main roads, often with road works. Then we have to cross a busy part that has steps going down immediately on the other side. Even for pedestrians and cyclists crossing here is dangerous, while for us it is more akin to ourselves down a big dipper blindfolded. We have to take the horses over one at a time and there is very little space to manoeuvre. There isn't even a sign to warn the lorry drivers that they need to watch out for pilgrims as they thunder round the corner.

Later, we stop off at a large flour mill to ask if they will sell us some oats, but the reaction is negative and unhelpful, which is disappointing in view of the positive reactions we have had before. So we scrape some of their spilled bran into a sack and enjoy a minor theft that makes us feel better. Then, not long after, our faith is restored in Najera where a French woman stops to talk to us. She is very interested in our horses and has just bought a Spanish horse to take back to France. From here we inevitably get into conversation about our experiences and we tell her about the difficulty we have in finding food. It is through this that we meet her friend whose husband keeps horses just up the road.
We are told to go to the last building on the left and ask for Rufino.

In Spain, news must travel faster than light, because Rufino is already waiting by the door when we get there. He knows what we want and asks if we would also like to see his horses. Bear in mind that we are standing in front of a building that looks like a bankrupt garage, and then imagine our reaction when he turns on the light to reveal the most beautiful Andalusian stallion I have seen. Three years old and kept in a dark corner and never ridden. When he says I can buy it I nearly say yes, but sense kicks in before it's too late. Then he takes us into another yard where there are more stables, this time they are jam-packed with ponies jostling for space and sweating in their own heat.

'What are these?'

He laughs. 'Meat. They are going to Germany next week.'

We buy a large sack of whole oats and leave. I know it's business, and people have to make a living, but the hard reality is difficult to take when it's shoved in your face.

Tonight the *albergue* is parish-owned, large, new, well built, well organised and … we have a room to ourselves! Only people who have spent eight weeks in dormitories, shared with a minimum of ten other people, can know what this means. As I come out of the shower, red as a lobster, but clean, Robert and Moya shout from the other end of the passage. 'Double-rooms. Don't expect us to be up at dawn tomorrow.'

Anyone other than a pilgrim would think he was suggesting some heavy nocturnal activity. We know he is talking about sleep, real sleep, without the dawn rustlings of the insane and sadistic, who believe that any later than five am. is midday.

The girls are not so well off in a piece of scrubland behind, but they are not tethered, which is much better. When I look at them sniffing through the plastic bottles and other debris, I wish I could read their thoughts. Do they find the daily change of scene unpleasant? Do they mind tip-toeing through human dross? They seem calmer and closer to us than they ever were at home, but perhaps they are just depressed.

HEALTH AND PERFORMANCE:

Gwen's back is improving.

Vasco's paw seems to be hurting him again and I have bound it up.

My piles are almost gone.

DONATIVOS

From its very beginning, the road to Santiago was a means of communication and cultural exchange. Commercial ventures were set up on the back of the pilgrim trade and nothing has changed in this respect, so I suppose we shouldn't be too surprised that it has been turned into a main highway for cars. We are more surprised that no alternative route has been found for pilgrims on foot or hoof.

Today, we are riding through an infinite expanse of harvested wheat and corn that exploits every corner of land. The vineyards are gone, and we are forced to walk alongside and sometimes over main highways. It is monotonous, noisy and uncomfortable and I'm about at the end of my tether when we hit the oasis of Santo Domingo de la Calzada. The plazas and churches and guidebook histories screech at us to stop and look, but we can't, and that is one of the difficulties of travelling with horses. Here, parking places for equines are in short supply and people don't like the piles they leave behind. So we have to go on to the next village, Granon, and find yet another oasis.

The *albergue* in Granon is called the hospital de peregrinos de San Juan Bautista and it is what is known as a donativo. Here, the old tradition of not charging still holds, and the collection box only asks pilgrims to 'give as much as you can or take as much as you need'. This is in the true spirit of the pilgrimage and the atmosphere is retained for the rest of the evening. We eat communally, while people play the guitar and talk. An older man, with an impressive white beard, plays traditional Spanish songs and I decide that I want to be Italian, because tonight they are in the majority and we feel like wooden dolls in comparison. We can't sing, we can't play an instrument and we sound like cracking coal when we speak.

For the girls, tonight's accommodation is not quite so charming, because they are tied up in a patch of rough scrub. The good news is that another angel has appeared to give us a sack of oats, so it's not all bad. It takes an hour or so of wandering around the village to find this particular celestial agent, but from there it is all very easy. We are taken to a large shed, where the young man opens the door on a huge mound of oats and fills our sack. Once again payment is refused, and we can only shake hands and mumble a pathetic muchas gracias. And what do you know? It's fiesta night tonight, again. Faye, our Canadian *hospitalera*, has warned us that it will be noisy. We don't care. Heard one, heard them all.

'Will the horses be all right?' She asks.

We laugh, and she no doubt thinks we're heartless, but by now they could probably tell her all about the Spanish fireworks routine.

Later, we attend Mass and decide the difference between here and Roncevalles is akin to the difference between a black and white photograph and actually being in the place itself. Like Roncevalles, the church is packed, the difference being that this time the majority of the congregation is from the village. There is one priest, as opposed to three, and every arch shudders under the power and emotion in his voice. Unlike Roncevalles, the congregation sings during the communion and doesn't need song sheets. As non-believers, Paul and I can only stand at the periphery and try to understand the faith behind the actions, but when, at the end of the service, Robert and some other pilgrims come from three aisles down to shake our hands and wish us peace, I feel that I am not far away. Outside, the rock festival has started up and another life is in full swing.

After a night on a wooden floor, with what Robert describes as mattresses of minus one centimetre thickness, getting up is a slow process. A creaking lethargy that is not helped by the weather - grey, overcast and distinctly cold. The landscape is still the same too, a monotonous vista of wall-to-wall harvested cornfields and I wonder how much longer the soil can last in this stripped and exposed state? On the way we meet up with Robert and Moya, who are having coffee in a village café. Robert's knee is causing him a lot of trouble, and Moya looks like she doesn't want to get up again, ever, but they laugh it off. 'It's because Moya and I are committed Catholics see. We reckon this pain will get us to heaven faster.'

'How much pain do you need for an express ticket?'

'Just about what we'll get walking from here to Burgos, then I'll have a hot bath and think of you guys slogging it up the trail.'

'Isn't schadenfreude a sin?'

'Yeh, but it's worth another half day's walk to enjoy it.'

Then Lubie dumps a pile on the pavement in front of the café, and I see the light.

I suppose I have been pretty tardy up to now when people complained about our horses and their habit of leaving a pile whenever and wherever the urge took them. It's probably because I have not done much urban riding, which is not an excuse. and today I feel distinctly guilty. At the next supermarket we buy a dustpan and vow to become responsible citizens. Why didn't I think of this before?

In the afternoon, the first *albergue* we try won't take horses, but the next one in Villa Franca Montes de Oca, an unpleasant strip of a village along the N120 road, seems surprisingly well organised in this respect. For twelve euros per horse (more expensive than our bunks) they are put in a proper stable and are given as much hay as they can eat. It makes us feel good to leave them comfortable like this and we are in the mood for celebrating anyway because we have just passed the one thousand kilometre mark. We are brought back down to earth with a thud when we see the *albergue,* best described as a poor man's version of the Gulag. The only restaurant we can find is for truckers who think pilgrim-squashing is a legitimate pastime. We eat a greasy tortilla and slink off to our bunks, with Vasco hidden in my coat. And guess what? It's fiesta here today. More fireworks, more heavy rock, more vomit on the pavements in the morning. The girls probably think that this is what humans do all the time.

Paul – One Thousand Kilometres

We have survived the *Camino* for more than fifty days and covered more than one thousand

kilometres, so I guess I can begin to call myself a rider, even if it is in the narrow context of the *Camino*. Lubie has continued to take care of me and give me an education in what I can expect of her, and so the process of improving my riding has been gentle and painless, if I discount those sore patches on my bum, and a dull ache from my knees to my hips that sets in towards the end of each day.

Green plastic phobia? I think I now have this sorted or at least understood. It is all to do with the sparrow effect. If you take time to watch a sparrow drink from a puddle, it is always alert to danger and the slightest unexpected event will set it in flight. This is much the way it is with Lubie. If something is not as she expects, then she is off. The good news is that she has a brain and what is new and therefore unexpected one day is old hat the next. All she needs is a few seconds to recognise that it is something she has seen before. So today green plastic is no longer a threat, nor are helicopters, Lycra'd mountain bikes, fireworks or bagpipes and marching bands. However, that vital second of recognition is still needed, so we tread warily near blind entrances that could conceal some threat she may not have time to recognise, or on those occasions when she lets me take control I try to distract her or hurry her on before she has the opportunity to consider the danger.

As we slowly eat away the kilometres it is clear that we are communicating in progressively subtler ways with direction changes and stops and starts happening through some evolving language of body movement, clicks and whistles. It is from somewhere in this process that my enjoyment of riding is growing. I do not think that the enjoyment comes from simply knowing that I am in control of a powerful animal, because of course I am not. At any moment she could decide to be rid of me and I would have no defence, it is more that we are finding that we can both get something out of the activity. This, perhaps, all comes together best when I feel a warm nose pressed against my hand or a playful nibble of my hair.

I think I am becoming more secure in the saddle since my early fall from Okapi. I know Lubie never has a deliberate intention to unseat me, but most days there will be some sudden movement and I will wonder how I managed to remain upright. Since entering Spain the horses have had to cope with increasing numbers of flies on their faces and bellies. As each day wears on Lubie becomes more exasperated with these pests and adopts all of Vasco's tricks to lose them, from the shake that starts at the nose and ends at the tip of the tail, to the scratch behind the ear with the hind leg. Surprisingly, sitting these out is now quite normal, and no longer accompanied by a string of expletives.

So, having started riding just five months ago, I think I have grown considerable confidence with Lubie. I am cautious that this does not become complacency, and still very aware of our limitations. None the less it really is fun and, as Babette keeps telling me, we have achieved things that more accomplished riders dream of, but I can only think: one thousand kilometres – bloody amazing!

This morning we are picking our way through the remnants of

the previous night's fiesta, trying to avoid the boys and girls still hanging over walls and benches like seaweed, both in colour and shape. It's cold, perhaps the coldest it's been yet, though our moods are lifted because the landscape has improved dramatically. We are out of the flat arable plains and making our way into the forests we have been seeing on the horizon for so long. Like coming home again: rough tracks, some steep climbs and most importantly of all, interest.
I walk as much as I can just to relieve Paul who insists on doing the most, but also just to get warm.

Mid-morning, and for the first time we find ourselves unwelcome in a village. When we tie our horses up outside a café, the owner waves us on and directs us to a signpost at the end of the road. Initially, I feel angry, then realise that we are at fault as much as the previous riders who have gone before us. Horse droppings, though marginally less rank than a dog's, are nevertheless unpleasant and should not be left to lie where it falls. Still, someone is up there and smiling on us, because just as a sharp drizzle starts we arrive in Ages, a small village with a large heart. We aim for the Caracole, a donativo *albergue* with an immediately welcoming atmosphere. Anja, its Swedish proprietor, tells us that the horses can either go in a small back room of the house, an outhouse that would have crumbled under one of Gwen's less offensive wind blasts, or on the village football pitch. We go for the safer option, though it does mean we have to tether the horses to the goal posts, which we hope is the opposition end in view of the souvenirs that the girls are sure to leave behind.

And it's fiesta time again, but with a difference, because this village does not want to just get pissed for a minimum of three days. No, Ages has taken on a medieval theme, with the villagers all dressing up in traditional clothes and the stalls selling ethnic and traditional wares. The atmosphere is refreshingly different from the usual brash blasting of the previous fiestas, and we are determined to appreciate the re-enactment of King

Alfonso's entry into the village, which to the uninitiated seems to involve a lot of people with pitchforks, knights on horses and a big chair wrapped in tin foil on a wooden stage. After that, an authentic medieval banquet is held, and true to form a great deal of mead or grog is drunk, with the result that all those ethnic types in sack cloth just become the usual crowd of piss-heads. This time we were pleased to be able to join them.

Burgos

August in Spain. Grey clouds and a sharp drizzle greet us as we ride out, but below, the views are stunning and through the mist we can just see the shadow of Burgos. Up on the summit we are one thousand one hundred and fifty metres high, and in the past this was known as one of the harder sections of the route for pilgrims. Aimery Picaud recalls in his second book of the *Liber Sancti Jacobi*, that a young, French pilgrim died here, and was later resuscitated, thanks to the protection of St. James, so that he could continue his journey. I can't say that we are suffering to anything like this extent. Our horses seem to positively enjoy the challenge of the climb, and I have ridden Gwen briefly without any obvious signs of discomfort, but I wouldn't say no to a small miracle if an extra coat could be made available.

We have been looking forward to seeing Burgos again after our very favourable visit last year, though as we ride into the outskirts it is hard to remember why. We trudge for what seem like endless hours on the edge of a very busy main road, while the traffic thunders past. Warehouses line each side and it is a soulless dispiriting place to be. The only aspect I can find cheering is that our horses do not seem in the least perturbed. They have come a long way since we started introducing them to cars and tractors on the small country lanes at home.

As we plod on, a car pulls up in front and a woman gets out. I think she is going to tell us that we can't walk there, so I'm trying to think of the Spanish for mind your own fucking business, but fortunately she is quicker off the mark than I am. She explains that if we try to walk into Burgos centre it will be very hard for the horses, and recommends we take a route along the river and inside the park. We are of course very grateful and try to follow her instructions. Ten minutes on we are dithering and cursing in front of a set of traffic lights.

'These ones or the next?'

'I don't know. You're the one who's supposed to be able to speak Spanish.'

She pulls up again, points to the next turning and then drives off again with a cheery wave. My mouth sometimes gets me into a lot of trouble, but this time it didn't. Thank you God, St. James and all the other saints I can remember from my convent days. I promise I'll be good from now on and say a Hail Mary. We find the park shortly after, and spend about an hour avoiding dogs and people who zig zag in front of us on the cycle path. We are heartily relieved when we see the Cathedral on the other side of the river.

Our Lady of Burgos was begun in the 13th century and completed in the 15th and 16th centuries. The entire history of Gothic art is summed up in its superb architecture and its unique collection of works of art: paintings, choir stalls, tombs and stained-glass windows. We know this from all we have read and the parts we saw during our previous visit, but this time it's impossible for us to do anything more than look from the outside, and hope that neither Gwen nor Lubie feel the need to do anything embarrassing on the marble flagstones in front. Then it's photos, photos, photos as we pose for ourselves and the hundreds of other people who ask us to. Exhilarating lunacy and, best of all, and hardest to believe, we have actually made it to Burgos, with two horses and dog.

When the German monk Hermann Kunig von Vach passed

through Burgos in 1495, the city contained no less than thirty-two pilgrim hospitals. Today we find only six listed in the book and not one of them takes horses. On top of that the signs for the *Camino* have completely disappeared and we whirl round manically while people point in a variety of directions in an attempt to help.

'Up there.'

No, that way is better for the horses.'

'But it's quicker there'

'Hey I know that bloke, let's follow him.'

Eventually, after a frustrating half hour of weaving in and out of the heavy traffic, we find the place we have decided might be more willing to accept horses, because it is in a park area and on the edge of the main centre. We are greeted by an elderly Spaniard who accepts them, but says they must stay outside the low wooden perimeter because he doesn't want any caca inside. Fair enough. We tether them as instructed and then go into see what the rest of the accommodation is like.

From my reading of the *Camino* histories, I understand that the hospitality and aid practiced within hospitals during the Middle Ages, was supposed to mirror the seven works of mercy – I feed, I visit, I water, I soothe, I clothe, I ransom, I bury. Something must have changed between then and now, in Burgos at least, because the only similarity I can find is in the obvious desire to bury any pilgrims who are unfortunate enough to stay here.

Perhaps the owner of this particular *albergue* used the plan of a prison to work from. Or maybe he thinks pilgrimages are 'only for professional travellers and rogues who, from superstition or debauchery, go to Our Lady of Loretto or Santiago de Compostela in Galicia, asking for alms on the way (Encyclopaedia 1735)'. Who knows? This is worst place we have ever stayed in.

Bunk beds are packed into every available space and next to each other without a millimetre of air between. A total of sixty people wedged into a garden shed. The walls are wooden, the windows are barred, and later we find that the door will be locked with everyone inside. Cheap it may be (three euros), but the lives of the people staying in there are not. In the showers the water is cold, the electricity is dodgy and the washing facilities for clothes so Spartan that in another situation it might have been funny. Then we meet the [19]*hospitalero*.

There must be something about the job, in the big cities, that attracts people with a power complex or ambition to be the next dictator. We've met a few before, though nothing on this scale. The Generalissimo answers our first question about where to put the tack, with a Spanish tirade, from which we are able to understand, more or less, that he has never had to deal with this problem before. What problem? All we did was ask where our stuff wouldn't be in the way. Then there is the tourist train, a freebie organised for the pilgrims by the Burgos tourist authority, except that he has taken it upon himself to inform us that Vasco is not welcome on it. We ignore him, while he watches us closely Though we do our best to comply with the usual dog-banning order when we go to bed, Vasco walks in through the still open door, prompting hysteria on the Generalissimo's part and badly suppressed laughter on everyone else's. Then it's lights out. Ten o'clock and most of us still only half undressed. Tough, because in this hut the Generalissimo is king of the switches.

Oasis

Six o'clock the next morning and the lights go on. Some of us may have wanted to sleep in, but our friend is not one for asking. We collect our tack and get out as fast as we can while I make juvenile, but very satisfying finger-gestures in his direction.

The road out of Burgos is resolutely flat and the distinctive Castilian [20] Meseta becomes wider and wider with only very slight undulations. More corn fields, more depressing because with the harvest finished it is an entirely dead landscape. On the hilltops, the trees have been stripped and the land is already desert. In the fields, the soil is so thin that it barely covers the stones that litter every inch of space. Am I sounding miserable? Am I complaining too much? You should try it one day. Then the sun comes out and our luck changes.

We moved into the thicker timber. The sun pierced the canopy of branches and spangled our shoulders with leaf-patterns. A cool leaf-mould breath rose from the foot-printed moss. The track dipped sharply down into a gulley and ended in a small clearing.

From These Are My People, by Alan Marshall

We have been travelling for the best part of four hours when we see Sambol resting in a valley off to the left of the track. A small building with flags flapping in the brisk breeze, and as we get closer I can see that two of them are proclaiming peace in Spanish. We haven't done the distance we planned, the horses are going well and showing no signs of tiredness, but this is my kind of place and we all need an antidote to the previous night, so we stop.

Paul speaks to the young Italian *hospitalero* and finds that he has no objection to the horses and is relaxed about Vasco. Things are looking up. We untack and find a place to tether the girls while we sort ourselves out, though it's clear that later we will be able to let them roam loose.

Sambol describes itself as an oasis and I can't think of a better word. A traditional domed tower in a grassy space, protected from the wind by a ring of ancient trees. A stream runs through the middle of a grassy area at the rear and feeds the only washing facility. The water is freezing, but when I compare it to the hole-in-the-ground toilet facility just beyond, I lose the will to complain.

'This reminds me of Glastonbury and when I used to go on camping trips with Lucy's school.' I reassure Paul, when he checks my face for the tell-tale signs of the 'you must be joking' variety. This time I really mean it. As we sit and watch the girls roll the sweat off the backs, the poison of the previous night drains away and I notice that someone is playing a flute nearby.

It doesn't take long to get to know everyone because it's a small place and people want to talk. We meet Stuart, our third English pilgrim since starting out. He was just passing through, but got hooked by the atmosphere and decided to stay. He's not the only one. This is the kind of place that attracts people with no timetable, or if they had one they've forgotten it, and I sense that we are not so far from doing the same. The girls will have their day off here.

As we exchange experiences it quickly emerges that the Generalissimo, our friend in Burgos, is as well-known as the place he manages. Another pilgrim we speak to tells us that he had made the mistake of getting up marginally later than the rest and found the washing facilities locked. Only a great deal of angry argument could persuade the old bugger to open the door, and then only for a grudging five minutes. Hearing this we feel slightly relieved to know that we are not the only ones to get on his wrong side, but actually does it matter? No, not any more, not when you can lean against a tree, shaded from the wind and in the warmth of the sun, with your horses roaming free only an arm's length away in the long grass. If the world wants to stop now, it's fine by me.

The next day we leave the girls to roam for hours at a time without any fear that they will go far. Gwen turns up to take a drink from the pool at regular intervals, and then goes off again with only the briefest of sniffs in our direction. I suppose she is just checking that we are still here and I regret that in spite of their perfect behaviour, we still don't have the confidence to allow them to roam as freely at night. We have found a derelict farm building nearby that we have roped off to avoid tethering. We wouldn't even need to do this if they were hobbled.

I hobbled the horses out on the plain that stretched to the horizon behind the camp.

From These Are My People, by Alan Marshall

My hero, Alan Marshall, used hobbles and because of this I have read about the different types and how to apply them and yes, I do know the theory, but putting it into practice is another matter. Images of Gwen falling again and again and again have become a regular nightmare, even though I have seen for myself that horses quickly adapt. My fear, though completely irrational and unproven, is preventing our horses from being free when they could be, so hobbles go on the list of things to do when we get back home, and I tell Gwen that everything will be fine. As we loll around reading and sleeping, we meet a couple from America who are on their pre-marriage honeymoon and still like each other after slogging along the *Camino* and wearing old socks. 'You can only say you know each other after a week of not washing.' We are told, though I beg to differ. On this basis Paul and I will never know each other, at least I hope not.

From our conversations we work out that they had set off from Le Puy en Velay just one day after us and have been following our horse droppings ever since. Their view is that travelling in Spain is far less easy, and a couple they had been travelling with have even decided to stop because they disliked it so much. This is a sentiment we can understand. There have been some uncomfortable and unpleasant episodes, Burgos being an example, but both Paul and I insist that nothing we have experienced so far has made us want to give up - a sentiment that is reinforced by saying it.

MESETA BLUES

The road ran through flat country cracked into jigsaw designs. The surface crumbled when you walked on it.
From These Are My People, by Alan Marshall

The wind drops and the sun decides to appear in full force on our third day in Sambol, a definite sign that we should be moving on. Gwen accepts the saddle without flinching and we have a very easy morning's ride through gently rolling countryside. The arable crops still predominate, but there are also some struggling fields of sunflowers to break the monotony, and we find the pretty village of Hontanas for our breakfast [21]bocadillo. This is an occasion that Gwen's belly has timed down to the last second, and she becomes increasingly stroppy if we happen to go through a village without stopping at the appointed hour. She is aided and abetted in this by Vasco, who appreciates the treat as much as she does, and will beg outside every café until we are worried that people will think we are starving him. Today we have the usual fight over who gets the tortilla and who gets the bread, while using the opportunity to ask if there is anyone here who could sell us some oats. Everyone tries to be very helpful, but we are told that we will have to go Castrojeriz, the next large town.

From here the road goes back to flat, flat and more flat, which makes the Castrojeriz castle ruins on a bare conical hill, appear to be even more menacing than its history. In the past this area was the scene of clashes between Moors and Christians and Castilians and Navarrese, which probably explains why the castle was already fortified by the ninth century. The village itself is pretty and well-prepared for the hordes of pilgrims that pass through. Every other house is a refuge of some sort or other and at the edge we find a grain store prepared to sell us some oats, which puts everyone in a good mood.

A few kilometres on, we cross the eleven-arch bridge over the River Pisuerga, which marks the border between the provinces of Burgos and Palencia, a notable point I am sure, though by this time we are more intent on finding a place to stay, and after Sambol I am insisting that it has a shower. I get better.
Tonight we are in a double room with our own bathroom and the girls are in the garden outside.

HEALTH AND PERFORMANCE:

Vasco's paw seems to be a great deal better though the claw has not come off yet

Gwen's back improving and growing hair. We will start to ride her for short distances

Lubie has developed a swelling on her back, which we think must come from the rolled tent resting behind the saddle. Gwen will take it tomorrow.

Paul's hip aching and very uncomfortable today.

Both Lubie's and Gwen's boots are suddenly showing signs of serious wear – we may finally be forced to look for a farrier.

I am energised by my plans to fight for cleanliness and safety on the St. James Way. Paul is probably sick of it already, though he is too kind to say so when I stop, yet again, to take another photo of pilgrim rubbish.

Lucy preparing for Lycée and being very efficient, but I feel left out and helpless.

Phoned Lucy last night and only got a drunken drawl in reply. Managed to deduce from this that a few friends are staying over and all the remaining wine from our barbecue has been drunk. Clearly she is having a good time and not missing us at all. I think I am pleased.

LOSSES:

A Ben Elton book that Paul was in the middle of reading.

Our indispensable collapsible bucket!! We think back and decide that it must have fallen out of a saddle bag. We won't be able to buy another here so we will have to resort to using plastic bags where there are only taps – which seems to be the case more and more.

Our Spanish dictionary and phrase book – though we have never used it.

A warmer day and a good start, though we are riding along an endlessly straight road through endless vistas of parched fields. The horses clearly hate it too and are finding any reason for stopping. I don't blame them and liken it in my mind to a life without cause or inspiration. Simple progression for the sake of progression, going nowhere without change and remaining unaffected by anything around. Perhaps this is my greatest fear, perhaps this is why Paul and I are always looking for something different, something to keep us occupied.

'Carrion de los Condes ... rich in bread, wine and all kind of products.' Amery Picaud's assessment is still a fair one, and our arrival here is only mildly complicated by the market that is in full swing in front of the hostel Santiago where we hope to stay, but the atmosphere is good. The owner of our hostel from the night before had recommended we come here and now we know why; it is a family concern and the family likes horses. Juan tells us with great pride that the previous week there had been eight of them here, and I imagine at the very least a stable block to take that many animals. I'm obviously a slow learner. When he directs us to the gardens of a Dance Hall and shows us how to shut the highly decorative wrought iron gates, I want to laugh. Our girls have experienced a thing or two during these last months, but this is a first. Paul and I scan the trees and undergrowth for anything poisonous or otherwise dangerous and, fortunately, it all looks fine. Better still, there is a grain store behind where we can buy some feed, so who's complaining? Certainly not the horses.

Today we have yet more monotonous landscape, though the temperatures are good for riding and we eat up the kilometres. We also have lots of what we call thinking time, if only because there is nothing else to do. We go back to our old theme; Paul saying that our collective moral conscience is disappearing and me saying we simply don't have the power to express it any more. A depressing conversation that fits the landscape and shows that we are not too old to want to make a mark in this world. Perhaps my opportunity will come in the form of being the most influential cleaning lady in Spain.

The rubbish has got to me and now I am saying that something has to be done and someone has to take responsibility. Pilgrims leave the picnic areas in a disgusting state and no one seems to care. Today, we pass one that is directly outside an *albergue*, but clearly the owners feel no responsibility for the state of it. I rant and rave, resolve to take photos and plan to go to the Spanish Tourist authority and see if I can invoke some action. The same will go for *albergues* that show no concern for safety, and roads that put the lives of pilgrims and drivers at risk. Gwen quakes under my new energy and Paul nods approvingly, if only to keep me quiet.

In San Nicolas del *Camino*, our *albergue* walls are made of adobe and I have to take a photo. I know it's pathetic, but even though we have seen a great deal of the stuff in the older buildings, this is our first modern version. We like its warmth and the way the light reflected from the mud and straw becomes a gilded yellow that even a Dulux dog couldn't imitate.

We leave the horses in a shady place, just off to one side of the football pitch, and Gwen finishes every last pellet of the Luzern she had sifted out of the corn just that morning. Perhaps this means that she is beginning to realise that she has to eat when she can and there is no room for fussiness on the *Camino*. Nevertheless, she still gives up on the tough, dry grass while Lubie scavenges continually. No wonder she has such a belly.

Within minutes of our arriving an old man takes up position in the nearby picnic area and assumes responsibility for them. When we come back half an hour later, another old codger is with him. An hour later there are four. I think we must have tethered our horses in front of their evening gossip spot, but they will be well cared for here.

Just as we are about to finish our meal, one of the old men comes up to tell us that a horse is loose. We run out to find that it is of course Lubie who is sprinting from one side of the football pitch to another in true trotter style. When she gets back to Gwen, where she should be, she lets herself be caught and tied up without any resistance, so I guess she just wanted to show us that she could still do it. The day ends in Vasco having to be locked outside in the garden, with no way that we can sneak him back in. I can't sleep and in the early hours he starts whining. We talk to him out of our window, it is all we can do. Today, Vasco is sulking, but only with me. I am to blame for making him sleep outside and I will be made to pay for it. He slinks off when I want to put him on the saddle, but when I get him he immediately falls asleep so he obviously had a bad night.

The road moved slowly beneath us, obscured by

the dust from dragging hooves. From These Are My

People, by Alan Marshall

The route is once again utterly boring and the girls are dragging their heads and heels like old donkeys, though they perk up briefly when we find a cereal merchant and are able to buy some corn. Then eventually, after a long slog through scrubland, we arrive in Calzadilla de los Hermanillos, where we put them onto a marsh area that is knee deep in the lushest grass they have seen since coming into Spain. All's well that ends well.

The village doesn't have a great deal to offer, other than the kindness of the people and the diversion of some sheep going through the middle. In the evening we talk to a Danish woman of sixty plus, who tells us that she customarily walks fifty to sixty kilometres a day, but the pack is slowing her down to about thirty. I feel totally pathetic and refrain from telling her about our aching legs and raw backsides. Mine, though I can't get round to see, must have blisters the size of eggs on it, and I wonder if I should treat them in the revolting way walkers tell me they do, by sowing a thread through to drain off the fluid. True love, is seeing your lover with threads hanging off her buttocks and sharing a bunk with her socks.

Pilgrims from Hell

We are woken by the pilgrims from hell, crashing every door and making every bodily function an event to be remembered. Is this an entirely Spanish phenomenon? I don't know, but they definitely take the first prize for decibels. We try to sleep, but give up by 6.30 and stumble out into the half-light.

Will the horses be there? Will they be all right? Have they got tied up? No matter how good our horses have become, the same thoughts rattle through my head every morning and for some reason I am even more worried this morning. Perhaps it is because of our bad night, or perhaps because there is the added risk of the swamp at the edge of the grass. I race down, but the girls greet me with the usual whinny and wonder what all the fuss is about when I throw myself round their necks. In fact, they have had a very good night. They have cleared every inch of grass and there is still more to have when we take them off the tether to tack them up.

The fun stops there, because this is just about the most boring stretch of the *Camino*, even though yesterday I thought I'd just been there. Hour after hour on a straight, stony track, through unremitting plains of harvested cereals. Perhaps it would not have been so bad if we had been able to trot and eat up some of the distance, but with our back-packs it is difficult, plus the state of the boots makes us reluctant to do anything more than a walk on the stony surface. Still, there is one highlight when an old man stops us on the track to give us some plums he has just picked, which helps to remind us of our status as pilgrims. We thank him inefficiently and then scoff them within five minutes, because this is breakfast.

From here we plod on, both horses looking and feeling more mule-like by the second and I can sympathise. I try to fill my head with useful thoughts, the thing that we are all supposed to do here on the *Camino*, but give up and let it fall into a blankness that matches the environment.

As is the custom now, mid-morning we hope to find a village where we can stop off for a coffee and a bocadillo. Here, the only one we can see from our map seems to have disappeared from the landscape, so we trudge on until we suddenly find ourselves in Mansilla de las Mulas, and life begins look as if it might be worth the effort.

This is where a 17th century traveller reported having seen wolves eating the corpse of a pilgrim, a piece of gruesome history I typically remember. Today, Mansilla de las Mulas is just a lively town and the *albergue* is in the middle of it. Better still, the horse accommodation is official and free. We are directed to a relatively derelict space that looks as if it must once have been some kind of animal market, but now the girls have got it all to themselves. They roll and cavort, both putting on a sprightly display in spite of the hard day. We leave them loose, reassured that they are both happy and safe.

Now it is our time – shower, beer, food and more beer, in that order. We investigate the town and I like it. History shouts from every corner; the medieval walls and gates, the arches of the Roman Bridge and its strategic position on the banks of the Esla. On the way I fall in love with an adobe house – do you think we could get a mortgage on that? Then we find the river and paddle with Vasco, after which we follow a crowd that seems to know where it is going.

I have neither seen nor heard of a Tomatino fight before, though

Paul tells me that this is what everyone is getting so excited about. My moral hackles rise. People are throwing tomatoes at each other. What a waste of good food! Some starving child in India could live of that for a ... We watch for a while and then head off for the tourist office to ask for help in finding a farrier, because the boots are finally about to give out. Asking for the moon, gift wrapped, would have been easier.

The woman wants to help, but her answer that today is Sunday isn't very helpful. Yes, we know, but could she possibly look through her yellow pages for the telephone number of a farrier so that we can phone tomorrow? A what? A veterinary clinic? No, our horses aren't sick, they just need new shoes. She explains this to someone who seems to be hanging on at the other end of a mobile phone in her hand. Whoever it is seems to have more sense and she comes back with the Spanish name for farrier, herrero, and suggests that she can look for this in the yellow pages. I refrain from saying that this is just what we have asked her to do and she finds one, though not in Leon as we had hoped. A buzzing comes from the mobile again and her face lights up. Of course there is a [22]Centro Hippico in Leon, we could go there. Brilliant idea. Could she find a phone number for it so that we could contact them before going there? Apparently not, but she shows us where it is on a map and we think we have a solution. We have succeeded with less information before.

As we leave the office we are stopped by a pair of German women we had seen booking into the *albergue* not long ago. They ask about our horses and whether we have experienced any particular difficulties, enquiring specifically about the stony track. We give them an overview and explain that in our view the horses would have suffered without the boots. They are interested and ask whether we had been able to use a guide book specifically for riders and when we say no, they tell us we should write one. What a good idea! I have lost count of the number of people who have said that it is their dream or plan to ride the *Camino* one day, but don't know how.

As we drink yet another glass of wine in another street café, a young and drop-dead gorgeous (sorry Paul, it has to be said) Italian man asks if we go fast on the horses. We tell him no, because we are here to appreciate the journey and he nods knowingly in reply, while pointing to his head and then his heart: "It is for these, not the walking." Only a gorgeous hunk of Italian could get away with it.

Later, a pair of slightly older Italian men, Alessandro and Lorenzo, who have waved at us before, stop to ask about Vasco and the horses. I recognise them, and realise from our conversation now that they must have been watching us for some time. They eulogise about the way Vasco placidly accompanies us wherever we go, riding or on foot, and I suppose now I come to think about it they are right.

Meanwhile he laps up the praise and doesn't let us down by humping their leg or peeing on the chair.

He is a very special little dog.

Our last task is to visit the girls and give them their evening feed. They are still content and Lubie is mooching around a derelict building that has all the signs of once being a toilet. She's not fussy, it's cooler. Then, we go back to the *albergue*, only to find the passages full of mattresses and worse still the pilgrims from hell in the room next to ours. We smuggle Vasco in as usual and hope that we have drunk enough wine to make us deaf to their morning clamour.

More Angels

We always said to each other, "Well, it's a certainty we will never meet so many kind people again," but we always did, and this surprised us until we realised that the only reason for surprise is when you meet the other kind.

From These Are My People, by Alan Marshall

Five o'clock and hell lets its pilgrims out. I question the need to scrape a chair across an entire room or drop boots from the upper bunk, but no one is listening, so we give up and get up, even though it's too early and we have to tack the horses in semi-darkness. Then it's back on to the boring bleakness of a stony track, made slightly more unpleasant than usual, because now we are riding parallel with a busy road. It gets worse when the track puts us on to the road itself and in one place over a treacherously narrow bridge where the lorries thunder past with only inches between us. In Spain we have already encountered a number of places where the *Camino* intersects with main highways, this is perhaps the most dangerous yet.

Whoever dreamt up the idea of directing pilgrims on foot (never mind on horseback) down the side of a busy dual carriageway, must either have a grudge against our dusty brethren or just gets off on being a sadist. As we try to find our way in the gutter, so that we are not walking directly in the traffic, the cars blare and toot to let us know it is madness to be there. I want to scream back that if we had a choice we wouldn't be there, fuckwits! Then, as we teeter between either a one-swipe-and-you're out kind of death or the more usual blood and guts all over the tarmac option, two words come to mind. Training and Trust. The TT factor. Or how else can I explain the fact that we are able to ride horses like ours through this torrent of motor madness? As I push Gwen over a slatted-bridge, through which the thundering traffic is clearly visible below, her back is rigid with fear underneath me, but as long I keep on talking to her she does not hesitate.

'It's all going to be fine Gwen …. oh fuck …. no I didn't mean that, it was just that really big lorry that …. fuck, fuck, and any other really bad word that comes to mind because I am …. shit! ….. scared. Good girl … walk on …. that's fine … I've probably just crapped myself … nearly there … oh please nearly there ….'

By the time we reach the other side, her nostrils are blood red and my hands are deeply scored from the pressure of Vasco's clinging claws. This is not an experience any of us wants to repeat, but we have done it together and they have learnt a few more … very bad …. words.

After that, negotiating Leon's daytime traffic is nothing, and by virtue of some bellowed queries from Paul as to the whereabouts of the Centro Hippico, we find it relatively quickly at the back of a vast yard of cars confiscated by the police. It doesn't look very encouraging. We dismount and Paul goes in search of someone to ask about a farrier, while I wait with bated breath.

When Paul comes back, he tells me that in spite of our initial impression, we have come to what looks like a very respectable stud. Santos, the owner, is wearing overalls and does not speak a word of English, but he does have a palmtop full of contacts and enough authority to be able call up the farrier on his mobile and tell us that he will be here at about five this afternoon. Then he points to a row of stables and suggests that we leave our horses there.

'What overnight?'

'Of course.'

'Can we pay you something?'

'No.'

Gwen and Lubie are led into luxury – automatic drinkers, deep beds, mineral blocks and real hay. An equine Ritz.

At five o'clock the farrier arrives and shortly after Santos is back too, without his overalls and driving a brand, spanking new Mercedes. Three hours later our horses are shod, with Santos acting as overseer throughout, and somehow managing to hold a conversation with us in our mixture of French and Spanish. Under his watchful eye, the farrier does a thorough job and tells me that their hooves are very dry. I know, but have had difficulty in using oil because it makes the boots slip off. No problem, I am told, just use water. This, for someone who comes from a temperate climate and is used to fighting foot rot, is a strange concept. He sees me balk and then smiles: 'Or use hand cream. It's more expensive, but works the same.' Yet another lesson learnt on the *Camino*.

While the farrier works, Santos shows me his horses which include a number of impressive Anglo Arabs, a Holstein stallion and a couple of Andalusian mares. He must have about twenty horses here, all beautiful, all ages from foal to fully grown, and he has another thirty or so on his farm outside Leon. He is obviously in the top league, but remains quietly diffident and keen to acknowledge our own importance as pilgrim riders.

Leon at night is like all cities in August, south of Watford. People eat and drink in the pavement cafés and we are just one more couple enjoying the atmosphere, though of course there is more and it has something to do with the architecture and the moment and the Spanish. Amazingly, amongst the milling thousands, we meet people we know: Alessandro and Lorenzo, who, before even saying hello, ask where Vasco is. The young German who had waved over to us as were leaving Sambol and I christened Peter, because he looked sweet enough to be Heidi's boyfriend. Actually, as he tells us now with tomato red cheeks (bless), Heidi, a.k.a. Gabi his girlfriend, is arriving tonight, so he won't be sleeping in the *albergue*. Good thing too. Snorts, farts and phlegm distribution are bad enough, but being kept awake by a night time tango is going just one hair shirt too far on this road to Santiago. On the more normal register, we also meet Faye, the Canadian volunteer *hospitalera* in Granon, who is now on her way home. Circles within circles, a human vortex, bringing us back to the *Camino* and the people we have met on it, even those we are trying to avoid, like the biker boys and the seventy k's a day group. Then we have to go back to the *albergue*. I'm feeling upbeat about tonight because it's been modernised, the showers work and the bunks don't sway like herons in the wind when I climb on to the top one. Of course there is always a downside and as usual, it or they in this case, are human.

It all starts when I want to take out my contact lenses and have a pee. I take my wash bag to the wash room, put it on a vacant sink and decide to pee first. Bad move, because Bitumen (my name for a German girl in her mid-twenties) has fallen in love with my sink. There are four others, but she has to have mine and I am sumo-wrestled out of the way.

"Hey!" It's not an impressive retort, but anything better I might have been about to say, stalls in my throat when I see Botulism. She must have been in the toilet next to mine, and now she is fixing me with a reptilian glare that could have killed cobras.

"Ist wass?" Which loosely translated means is there a problem you need dealing with? Shall I duff her up?

Who? Me?

I don't actually say anything, but I do pick up my wash bag and stomp forcefully across to the other line of sinks. Well, there were two of them and they're both bigger than me.

When I try to tell people about Leon, I find it impossible to describe, because its impact hits us on so many levels; a merging of the historical and contemporary into a unique melange of culture and human energy. As we walk through the narrow streets with our horses, I see Alfonso III's momentous push for development and it is easy to understand why his successor, Ordono II, was able to proclaim Leon the most important city in Christian Spain (even though much of this was based on pinching each other's saintly relics).

When we pass the San Isidore basilica my mouth opens wide enough to let a swarm of bluebottles and their grandchildren in, and then there is the Gothic cathedral with its incredible expanse of stained glass windows, not only staggeringly, mind blowingly beautiful, but also incredible when you think it was all started in 1063. We can't even build a house without the plaster cracking today, so how did they manage this?

And what about the Hospital of San Marco? Built by the order of Santiago at the beginning of the 14th century and converted into a Parador good enough to get the 'when I'm rich and famous' treatment from me. Actually, it is the statue of St. James himself that I find the most impressive, a life-size rendering that stares up at the vast face of the Hospital and says more than any words can. It doesn't matter that his presence here is probably entirely mythical, or that the man himself could never have done even half of what they say, because for me this is quite simply man or woman, me, staring up into the sky and asking the simple question: How did we get here and why?

Meanwhile Lubie and Gwen are making the most of their own semi-mystical experience: ground level geysers of water that they can stick their noses in and blow bubbles through, again and again and again. Amazingly no one objects.

If you have managed to stay with us this far, you will know that of course nothing ever goes quite according to plan. As we follow Leon's brass *Camino* cockle shells into the centre, our perfect progress is suddenly brought to a skidding halt when Gwen, in her new iron shoes, slides Bambi style on the marble flagstones. We have negotiated the cobbles well enough, but within seconds of entering the cathedral plaza, the girls are literally skating. We dismount nervously and stop briefly to let some people take photos of us, then get back on the *Camino* where the horror has only just started. We are sent down one way streets the wrong way, and up to every monument that exists in Leon, which is a good idea if you are on foot, but hell on earth for us, with our horses in their slippery iron shoes. It takes three hours to get into the suburbs, where we are confronted with yet more traffic.

The horses slog on, obediently ignoring the huge lorries that thunder by, but just like us they are hating every minute. Having left the city, our intention had been to take a quieter, alternate route, but unfortunately someone, (perhaps the manager of the new *albergue* in Villadangos del Paramo) has carefully obliterated all the other arrows with his own promotion material, meaning we are forced to negotiate the N120, a major national highway with no time for pilgrims.

Information about the new *albergue* is painted on every available surface: walls, fly-overs, the road itself - graffiti on graffiti. It is ugly and unnecessary, but as this is a municipal *albergue* I suppose there is no one to whom we can complain. When we reach Villadangos del Paramo the *albergue* is all too obvious, while the accommodation for the horses is not. Nevertheless, one of our angels pitches up just in time, and while Paul is desperately trying to negotiate something, an elderly woman and her daughter walk over to me and point to a flat piece of green just fifty metres away. 'You can put your horses in there.'

I want to kiss her, but just say thank you in my hopeless Spanish.

BIRTHDAY

The early pilgrims may have faced all kinds of hardship and adversity much tougher than ours, but they didn't have the N120. As the guide book says, it has basically covered the original route in tarmac and trucks, and there has been very little effort to replace it with something preferable for the foot or hoof slogging pilgrims like us. We have been following this road for three days and the incessant noise and risk of the passing traffic is worse than the persistent bedroom mosquito. The horses hate it, and though today they seem relatively keen at the outset, their heads are hanging within minutes of hitting the highway. At various points we are forced to cross the road, putting ourselves and the drivers at very real risk and in fact I am just about to call a halt to the whole day, when we come to the bridge entering Hospital de Orbiga.

The bridge appears out of the blue, utterly picturesque and utterly out of place after the endless N120. A cobbled roadway over numerous arches spanning what must have once been a very large and healthy river, though it is little more than a trickle now. Then, just as we are scanning the horizon for a suitable *albergue*, we hear a shout from a balcony ahead. Allessandro and Lorenzo, plus some other German girls we have become on nodding terms with recently, are all standing up and waving.

'Hey! Where's the dog?'

'Why he not riding now?'

'How far you going today?'

'No further,' I reply. 'We're just doing a short day.'

'Why? Is problem with the horses?' Allessandro asks with concern written all over his face.

'No.' (Would he be as concerned about us?) 'It's Paul's birthday, so we're going to take it easy and celebrate.'

Enough said. Or perhaps I shouldn't have said it, because suddenly the bridge is reverberating with the sound of six people, singing Happy Birthday in a variety of versions and keys. The noise goes on until we have ridden across all twenty-four arches and the small town of Hospital de Orbiga can be in no doubt that we have arrived and that it is Paul's birthday. And, the good news has only just started. Next, only minutes after we have said goodbye to our personal choir, and seconds after I have thought that it is time for us to start scouting around for a field, a sprightly, elderly woman comes out of a shop and asks us in a volley of Spanish if we need anywhere for the horses. Does the pope ....?

We follow our Senora de los Caballos to a house that is fronted by a river and was clearly a working mill not so very long ago. In our terms perfectly idyllic: shaded, surrounded by grass literally dripping with lushness and about five minutes from the town. Then she gestures to a barn and asks us if we want avena (oats) or cebada (barley). This is too good to believe, not only is there food for the horses, but we are also given a choice. When we go inside the barn she gestures to two piles of hay: 'Alfalfa or grass, take your pick.' The charge for all of this is 16 euros.

After this kind of luck and luxury for the horses, we need to find something of a similar standard for ourselves, it is Paul's birthday after all. We take a look at the hostel we have seen on the end of the bridge and go budget-crashing mad - a double room with bath, the third since starting out from Le Puy en Velay.

The view from our window is directly over the bridge and, rather inappropriately for two old farts still in love and wanting to stay that way, we learn that the Hospital de Orbiga's famous jousting story was sparked off by a knight who wanted to dump his lady.

Suero de Quinones thought he could do this by organising a tournament and offering up as a prize, the gilded silver necklace he wore every Thursday in her honour. A simpler option might have been to quietly throw it in the river, but Suero was obviously a man who enjoyed the big public statement, so he arranged a tournament and swore to stop (with the help of nine other knights – clever man) any knight who dared to cross the bridge. After thirty-two days, including a rest on St. James's Day, seventy knights had taken up the challenge, with one even dying after receiving a lance in the eye. At the end of the tournament, all the knights (excepting the one who died, I presume) from both teams went to Santiago, where Don Suero presented his necklace to the apostle and where it still is today. A good story, but Paul and I don't plan to follow his cue, however badly we fall out.

Later, we go back to the girls and take them into the river where we soak their feet as directed by the farrier and Lubie splashes so furiously that we are soaking wet by the time we are ready to go for the birthday meal. As we are leaving, our Senora de los Caballos comes back from church in her Sunday best, and I decide that this is probably a good time for the photos. I ask her if she would mind standing with Lubie and Gwen, because I think it would make a cute picture: little old lady trembling nervously between our towering, snorting beasts. Then I stand back to take the photo and Gwen does her usual don't leave me on my own routine, but from here it is difficult to decide who is the more surprised, me or my horse. Just as Gwen takes a step forward, her head is jerked back with a force that would have broken a smaller horse's neck, while Paul and I look at each other in humble amazement. Our Senora de los Caballos knows what's she's doing and she isn't going stand for any messing around from a great hairy lummox like Gwen. She jerks the rein once more and gives me a dentured smile.

"Ahora, (now) foto. Ahora."

Just like Gwen, I don't argue and do as I am told.

HEALTH AND PERFORMANCE:

Gwen's back looks slightly swollen so we won't ride her tomorrow.

Both horses showing signs of feeling the stones on their soles - the Catch 22 of using boots, because the protection they provide actually leaves horses more sensitive when they are not being used.

Both horses look like they have put on weight – though of course Lubie more than Gwen

Vasco's paw is completely fine now that the broken claw has fallen off

Met a German last night who told us about a cream cyclists use for their sore bottoms. We will see if we can find the same. Paul also had the brilliant idea of wearing cycling shorts with the sewn in gel pads under our riding trousers. Bit late now, but may be good for the next long distance trip.

GOODBYE MESETA. GOODBYE N120

The road rollicked over hill after hill, challenging me at each crest to chase it to some culminating place of rest farther beyond the rise.
From These Are My People, by Alan Marshall

We have left the N120 and suddenly being on the *Camino* is fun again. We proceed through terrain that rises gently into the next range of hills, Los Montes de Leon, but comfortably so. The cereal wastelands are receding and here there is a more varied agriculture. This may be because the soil is too poor for the larger agricultural concerns to exploit – the soil is little more than dust – a negative aspect that may in the long run be its salvation. Trees have been planted and there is clearly an attempt to halt the erosion.

As we come over the brow of a hill we spot a familiar sight – St. John in his huge white camper van. He is serving coffee to a small group of pilgrims, including Karin, an Austrian woman we have met a number of times now, but stops to greet us like long lost friends, and then breaks into song:

'Happy Birthday to you, Happy Birthday ....'

News travels fast on the St. James Way.

As always John is full of useful information and chocolate biscuits. 'Here have some more ... take one for your dog ... you'll find a number of good *albergue*s for your horses ... what you don't feed them wheat ... there was a man with a donkey who ... let me get a cup of coffee ... how far are you going today ... photo .... of course ... biscuit ... coffee ...'

'Yes John, thank you John.'

Since yesterday life is really beginning to look up and Paul decides that being a year older isn't so bad either. Astorga is one of those towns that score high in terms of atmosphere and welcome. Our first encounter is the impressive Town Hall where photographs are obligatory, but the cathedral is something else – on the scale of Leon in a town a quarter of its size. Paul and I stand in awe and consider going inside, only to find that it is, of course, closed. We are disappointed, though not very, because the first traces of religious relic fatigue are setting in. Seen one, seen 'em all. Without reading the mounds of historical literature that goes with all the buildings we pass, we can only see them out of context and as flying buttressed wiggly bits of stone, with a mixture of tortured and beatific faces looking out from the crevices in between. Nevertheless, Astorga will stick in our minds as yet another place that we must return to, with the guidebook. This could become a life's time quest.

Later, somewhere out in the sticks, we spot two figures hunched like vultures over a carcass. Bitumen and Botulism are having a lunch break and, ever hopeful, I wave and wish them Buen *Camino* in true pilgrim style. They don't reply, but I'm sure I heard something that sounded very much like a low growl. Perhaps I've misjudged them. Perhaps they're not human at all.

The *albergue* John has recommended most highly is on the other side of Astorga and, just like the town, it gets a good score in our plebeian's book of Nice Places to Visit. Someone with a good eye has renovated it in the kind of traditional way that people like me, the Germans and the Dutch, will like. Even better, the *hospitalero*s like horses. An old man, the owner as we find out later, comes out and immediately comments on Gwen's size and strength, rather than Lubie's beauty. It is not often I want our horses to be able to understand human-speak, but now I wish she could. As someone who knows what it is like to be referred to as having a lovely personality (as opposed to a beautiful body or fantastic face), I know just how much this comment would mean to her. Following this, he brings out water and then offers to go into Astorga to buy oats for them – almost too good to be true.

Soon after, I get into conversation with a German (no I am not prejudiced, there are just more of them) woman who has got stuck in this area for six weeks, unable to go back to her previous life because of her various experiences on the *Camino*. I find this interesting and we talk about motives and such like, until she tells me that she was a druid in her past life and likes sleeping in caves, which is when I remember I have some washing to do. No, I'm not being cynical, I have done Stonehenge and Glastonbury when they were still 'real', but this woman is just barking mad. Fortunately, Karin turns up at about this time and comments that she knows enough about horses to know that our girls are well looked after, because they are shining and in good condition. She may be barking mad too, though she hides it well, and I prefer the things she says. Karin and I then spend the rest of the evening engaged in loud, Germanic hysterics, discussing our new found ability to identify sleeping bags by the sound of their zips at dawn, and the merits of Velcro as an instrument of torture.

HEALTH AND PERFORMANCE:

Gwen's back is looking considerably less swollen after today's short and riderless day. Perhaps we have got it back under control. Paul's bum better for the rest too.

LOSSES:

Yet another bottle of shampoo and two more pairs of knickers – where do they go?

HEADING FOR THE HILLS

Today we leave the *albergue* with hugs and best wishes from the *hospitaleros*. Vasco has won their hearts and he is outrageously spoiled in the last remaining minutes left to him. This is another *albergue* that deserves ten out of ten for its atmosphere and facilities. The girls are given a large breakfast of oats and then it's back on the road again.

Life is looking up in every respect since leaving Leon. In terms of our height, because we are beginning the steady ascent to 1500 metres before we reach Ponferrada, and also in terms of the landscape. We are now going through a mixture of coniferous and deciduous forests that break up the plateau expanse and make every minute of the walk a pleasurable experience. The only shadow is historical, but it is no less terrible for all that and exercises our minds on the inhumanity of humanity. On the slopes of the Aquilian Mountains that we are admiring for their beauty, slaves were put to work for over three centuries, sieving three hundred million tons of soil to enrich Rome by a million kilogrammes of gold.

Paul is on foot again, though Gwen's back has improved considerably. This is a precautionary measure (we will have about 30 kilometres to do tomorrow) and a macho statement (he claims to find walking easier than I do). Perhaps I should argue ... but then again perhaps not. As we discuss our plans for the next few days it occurs to me that we are less than two weeks away from

Santiago and I have mixed feelings. I don't want our adventure to end. The experience is addictive and I will find the sudden emptiness of our return journey hard to manage. On the other side, I want to reward the horses with a well-earned rest and some parts of our equipment, particularly the saddle bags, will only last another few days. Also, with September, autumn approaches and the cold weather that would make our journey extremely uncomfortable.

As we ride, we pass a large number of pilgrims who all seem to be heading for Rabanal del *Camino*. There are some familiar faces and just as many new ones. The majority are interested in the horses and enthusiastic about our journey, but one couple is less favourable: Madame and Monsieur Merde. They are in their mid-forties and in her case, quite well turned out (fashionable hair style and make up – how does she do it?), while their equipment indicates that they are familiar with walking. We pass them once or twice and on the way see her coming out from behind a bush where she has obviously been to relieve herself. Then later, just after going through a village with a number of cafes, we see him going behind a wall with a wad of toilet paper, clearly with the same intention. I am outraged and find it difficult not to say anything. If people are expected to clear away their dog and horse shit, then surely humans should do the same.

Rabanal del *Camino* is our goal for today and it is no disappointment. At the foot of the Montes de Leon range, it is a village of cobbled streets and thatched roofs that has developed considerably as a result of the recent pilgrim trade, but still manages to retain a great deal of its authentic atmosphere, some of which can be attributed to the strong Templar presence in the 12th century. Our hope is that we can stay in the famous Refugio run by the Confraternity of St. James, though unfortunately there are only twenty-four places and no facilities for the horses, so Paul asks an old man if he can help and we are immediately shown to a field where we can tether them. I thank him and he kisses my hand. Oooh...

Later, when we book into the Municipal *albergue*, the hospitelera, a very helpful local woman, tells us that she can organise a much closer field for the horses and so we bring them down. There is not much grass, but it is infinitely better, because they do not need to be tethered. She also says that Vasco can stay with us, officially, which is only the second time in Spain that this has happened.

As we go in to claim our bunks, we see some familiar faces. Where's the dog - Alessandro and Lorenzo, Madame and Monsieur Merde and best of all, Bit and Bot, in top form and full character. Bitumen stomps out of the bathroom just as Botulism informs me that it is occupied. If I hadn't seen them being equally unfriendly to other people, I might take their behaviour personally and assume they hate the English, or horse riders, or people with brown hair and a dog, but I have seen them apply their vitriol with exemplary equality to everyone they meet. Maybe they just hate people, the *Camino* or perhaps the whole world. If they were dressed in black and displayed some sort of youthful anarchy, I could, perhaps, accept their behaviour with a rueful, I was young once, kind of tolerance, but they make my grandmother look cool. Bitumen wears dresses that charity shops wouldn't even offer up as curtain material for the local Rest Home, and Botulism's sandals must have belonged to Lady Baden Powell. Wait and minute! What do they or the Merdes matter? We have just had a good meal, we are both in good moods and better still, Paul tells me, the bunks don't smell of dead bodies, so on this basis we can look forward to a good night's sleep.

Dawn and we feel like death. The pilgrims from hell are the heavenly twins when compared with this man. Phlegmkinstein starts with snoring. Loud, annoying, but tolerable if only because we are becoming immune to the row. Then he follows with the throat, or more specifically the clearing of the throat.

Gut-clearing echoes. Not once, not twice, but all night with insistent regularity. Does he really need to do this? Is he ill? If he is, why doesn't he consider the effect of his illness on other people and either go outside or pay the extra for a single room in a hostel? Hey! We would pay for you! Phlegmkinstein does not care, as is only too clear when he turns the dormitory light on at six o'clock this morning. Perhaps he assumes that by keeping everyone awake all night, we won't object to being roused at dawn. He is wrong. I am close to murder and disbelieving glances are exchanged across the room, but what is the point in protesting? It's too late. We are awake and won't go back to sleep now, so we get up and prepare the girls slowly, waiting for the sun to rise so that we can see our way out.

From here everything is pure gold, literally, as the sun breaks through and paints the tips of the grass on the slopes ahead. This is perhaps one of the most pleasant rides we have had since coming to Spain. We are riding up Mount Irago to the Cruz de Ferro in the abandoned village of Foncebadon, 1490 metres high. In the past, every stone piled up at the base of the cross had been left by Galician peasants on their seasonal trips to Castile for the harvesting. Now the pile has been considerably added to by the thousands of pilgrims who pass by every year, which I would have known if I had read the relevant books. Instead I only catch up with the history when St. John includes it in his 'must-know' local information, and now I insist that we pick up a couple of stones on the track before we arrive. Tradition says that the stones you lay should be an identification of past sins and a request for forgiveness, but Okapi with both packs full to bursting wouldn't be able to carry the number of stones
I need to appease my guilt, so I settle for three and write our names on them: Lucy, Paul and Babette.

Since setting out in the morning, the girls have picked up and shown willing after their head-dragging mope of the last few days. It's great to feel them enjoying the ride, but then we have a very difficult descent, made harder, much harder by the iron shoes. Whereas we would have taken the stones and steep incline in our stride before, now we are forced to dismount and it is clear that the girls are increasingly cautious. When we reach the bottom, a number of people comment on our arrival with amazement. They had assumed that we would have to take the cycle way.

We wanted the road to continue through a land of birds, but

we came to houses ... From These Are My People, by Alan

Marshall

After this everything goes literally downhill, the mountain and our fortunes. We decide to make the extra kilometres to Ponferrada, specifically because the guide book tells us that the *albergue* welcomes horses - a good opportunity to reward the girls with an open field and some food - when we get there it is a very different story.

No facilities for horses, no interest in making any facilities for horses, and a German volunteer of three days swamped with people coming in and no idea of what to do. We are told there is patch of ground at the back of the *albergue* where people do put their horses, but it belongs to the town and the *albergue* takes no responsibility if we are pushed off.

With no other alternative we go and look at what is on offer. The ground is a waste land. Filthy, no grass and only one area of shade where a small hut has been built, meaning we can't tie the horses there. Then we find that the volunteer is not willing to unlock the gate between *albergue* and the land – meaning we are unable to water the horses. When I get angry in my best and foulest German, I am told that maybe a key can be found, but I will have to wait.

We wait, and in the meantime arrange two bunks for ourselves with another volunteer. Half an hour later a key is found and we are able to settle the girls in. Then we go to our bunks only to find that they have been given to someone else and the alternative is to take the basement – a cavern filled with fifty beds and filthy sheets and …. Phlegmkinstein. But, as we invariably find in even the worst of situations, there is always someone on hand to restore our faith in humanity. This time it is the most long-term (two months) volunteer, who apologises for our treatment and subsequently drives Paul round the town searching for oats, eventually tracking down a riding stable that is prepared to sell some.

With all the ugly business out of the way, we go into the town and find that we have arrived in the middle of yet another fiesta. How do we do it? This time, instead of the noise until five in the morning, we are treated to an excellent display of regional folk dancing and music from a number of groups in the main plaza. Then we return to the *albergue* and break the news to Vasco that he will have to sleep outside. I feel terrible and wrap him in a horse blanket with a promise to visit him later. In fact, I fall asleep, and if Phlegmkinstein was active I was too tired to hear him.

Lights on at six o'clock, because we have to be out by seven thirty. This is the St. Nicolas *albergue* regime and while it may suit the majority of insanely early risers, it is no good for us when we can't leave with the horses until it is light. Still, it does mean we have more time to comfort Vasco and beg his forgiveness. The girls have survived their night, even though we find Lubie with the tether rope round her neck. We tack slowly and talk to Peter and Gabi, who tell us that they had managed to get a good room for three euros in the donativo *albergue* whereas I had stupidly, voluntarily, donated twenty euros for a stinking cellar. They commiserate and admit to only walking ten kilometres the day before, because they were very tired. I refrain from asking why, but presume their thirty kilometre target for today might have something to do with the fact that last night

Riding the Milky Way

they had to share a room with five other pilgrims. Peter is obviously into more than just goats.

Leaving Ponferrada is a slow business. With their new shoes the horses slide as if on ice and we have to dismount and pick our way carefully, but once we are outside and through the messy collar of urbanisation, we are rewarded by the tumbling vistas of vineyards that produce very good del Bierzo wine. Now we are surrounded by ranges of mountains and the *Camino* traces a gentle curve in and out of the valleys between them. We are climbing steadily, nothing too harsh and the descents on the wide and comfortable track cause none of the difficulties of the day before.

Less pleasant is a rather strange encounter with a family we have been doing our best to avoid for the past three days, mainly because they have dammed themselves in my eyes by allowing their twelve-year-old son (now dubbed Crapping Junior) to shit in the woods, just half an hour after starting out. Now, quite suddenly on the edge of a busy road, we are hailed by the mother and asked in rapid Spanish, if her son can sit on Gwen for a photo. I do my best to explain that this is not a good place and suggest we do so later in Villafranca del Bierzo, but the offer is not good enough. She wants it now and points to a wider place at the top of the hill. I shrug and indicate that I will have a look, pushing Gwen into a fast walk that I know they cannot keep up with, though Gwen has other ideas.

For people who know horses well, I don't need to explain that it is rare for them to pee on tarmac, preferring straw or something soft that will absorb the splashes. So, from what happened next I can only assume that she was either desperate or very literally pissed off. Anyway, whatever her motives, Gwen stops abruptly, straddles her legs in best mare style and lets out a volley of steaming piss and reverberating farts, within less than a metre of Crapping Junior. He is stunned, but his mother's face is a picture of incredulity and disgust. She probably thinks Gwen does this kind of thing on command and in a way I wish she did, but this time her behaviour was completely spontaneous, though perfectly timed.

After a pleasant five hours riding, we arrive in Villafranca del Bierzo, where legend has it that if a pilgrim could not carry on to Santiago, he could pray to be excused from further journeying without renouncing the benefits of his pilgrimage. Nice thought, except that unfortunately this clause was rendered null and void by a 1960-ish Pope who decided that walking this far along the *Camino* wasn't enough of a penance to give you a blank sheet so that you could start sinning again without losing your licence. What made him think he had the right to decide this is questionable, but it was probably the same divine right that said walking the entire *Camino* could give you one in the first place.

From here, we find ourselves in an excellent *albergue* where, apart from Crapping Junior and family, we are surrounded by pleasant people and the town itself is both attractive and has a good atmosphere. We are in a good mood and I finally allow Crapping Junior and his elder brother to sit on Lubie with Vasco in front. Numerous photos are taken and everyone is content, though interestingly no one asks if they can sit on Gwen.

On the way back from our evening meal, Paul and I are walking down a narrow track running below where the girls are tethered. It is about 300 metres away and we are in shadow, but it is enough for Gwen to see us and bellow her usual greeting. She's done it again, melted my heart, our ugly, clumsy, problem-prone mare, who knows just how to remind me that she is worth every second of frustrated patience and forbearance.

Kim was more than just a dog to us. He was the pattern of our lives … He was never depressed as sometimes we were. The wettest day could not damp his enthusiasm.

From These Are My People, by Alan Marshall.

Then we have the problem of smuggling Vasco in. The usual tur obenfuhrer (Paul's name for the many dog-phobic *hospitaleros* we have met in Spanish *albergues*) is sitting at her desk in the entrance hall, so we decide to wait until she has locked up and gone home before sneaking out and sneaking Vasco back in, but he has other ideas.

After the previous night in Ponferrada, he knows what being wrapped up in the horse blanket means and this time he is having none of it. He waits until we are upstairs and the woman is looking the other way, or at least we have to assume that this is what he has done, because suddenly he is at the foot of our bunk (no doubt easily located by the familiar pungency of our socks) and waiting to be hidden under the sleeping bag as usual. In the morning, as soon as the lights are switched on, he performs the same trick in reverse and before we have even begun to get dressed, has slipped out of the front door to sit on his blanket outside with a Who me? expression written all over his canine features. The boy is no fool.

HEALTH AND PERFORMANCE:

Gwen's back is definitely under control and on the way to recovery, though her weight loss continues to worry me.

Both girls are going extremely well and are clearly happy to be off the roads and roadsides. They are noticeably cautious on the tarmac and I can't wait to get the boots back on. How did I ever ride before?

Honey, gold and silver

On leaving the borders of Leon and the mountains behind, one is now virtually in Galician Territory with plenty of white bread, cider, milk, honey, gold and silver.
Aimery Picaud

Getting back on the road again feels good, but unfortunately it is literally back on the road. An extra piece of yellow tarmac running along the safe side of the crash barrier of the N6 for about 20 kilometres. Here in the region of Bierzo it is clear that where there is no alternative for the *Camino* to run, the authorities have made every effort to provide pilgrims with a safe channel. Signs warn drivers that pilgrims are there and make special efforts when there is a crossing point. How much better this is when compared with our terrible experiences on the outskirts of Burgos and Leon. Another improvement is the rubbish, or its lack. Perhaps it is because there are more rubbish bins around, so that even the pilgrims who would normally dump their cans and bottles where they stand, find that the one step towards a bin takes no effort. But, as there seems to be less toilet paper and sanitary towels around too, I suspect that the Galician authorities are simply more vigilant.

An unpleasant aspect of both France and Spain is that the majority of farmyards are stocked with a variety of dogs, some the size of rabbits and some that could look down on a Great Dane. Irrespective of size or breed, if they are loose they will lunge at the horses while Vasco guards them with every cell in his tiny fox terrier-ish body. Today is no different, except that this time one of the larger versions turns on him with real viciousness and Lubie, who usually treats Vasco with utter contempt, lunges forward to protect him. The dog-monster doesn't know what has hit him (it's Lubie's nose) and doesn't hang around to take a second look, but he will probably think twice before attacking anything else if there is a horse nearby. For me, this powerful expression of team spirit is twice as significant because it has come from Lubie, our equine ice-maiden.

Meanwhile, the weather is closing in, dark clouds are hanging over the mountains that surround us, and there is very little view of the sun all day. By the time we have ridden to the top of one particular peak, we are both frozen and tired, so Marcelino's bar catches us at just the right time. It may have been the offer of a glass of wine, or the Indian trinkets he had on sale outside, or the Tepee. The clincher is when he tells us that he has horse-feed he can sell us and a field for our girls. Say no more. We're staying. We untack, drink the wine and then put them in a shed mainly taken up by an old car, which has a manger-full of walnuts. Do horses eat walnuts? Well, apparently they do. I am initially alarmed and rush to pull their noses out, but when Marcelino tells me that his horses have eaten them for years without any problems, I let them have a go.

We leave them to crunch on and they seem content for us to go, so we drink more wine and while we talk a familiar voice addresses us. It's Joel, the Italian who speaks English with an Irish accent and as I now I learn, also perfect French and Spanish. He tells us that he has picked up a few days' work with Marcelino and may go on the next day or maybe not. I am fascinated by this man, a professional tramp by his own proud admission, who has as many nationalities as spicy roll-ups, speaks six languages without any hint of a foreign accent and has never stayed anywhere for more than six months at a stretch.

They heard me coming and whinnied a welcome. I stayed with them a little while, feeling troubled that they should have to stand out there alone in the cold and dark when we were warm in bed.
From These Are My People, by Alan Marshall

After the evening meal with Marcelino and Joel, Paul and I take the girls down to the field where Marcelino's fat mare lives with a donkey that was left behind by a French pilgrim the year before. Both object to the newcomers and the mare is particularly dominant. Poor Gwen, who is already bullied by
Lubie, clearly can't cope and after a forceful kick on her rump refuses to go back in until I coax her. Then she whinnies pitifully as we leave and I feel terrible, because I haven't the strength of character to override Marcelino's insistence that they are better outside than in the tiny stable. It may be the rain on the tepee roof that keeps me awake, or perhaps the thought that the girls have only a few trees to shelter under, but my head is spinning with thoughts of the catastrophes that could befall our beloved horses and my guilt in having left them there.

LAND OF CONTRASTS

The people are, before all other uneducated peoples of Spain, those who are closest to our French race by their customs, but they are, it is said, quick to anger and constantly bickering. Aimery Picaud

As we ride through rich valleys surrounded by high mountains, I try to put myself in the place of pilgrims in the tenth century and imagine that this area must have seemed like a green paradise after the barren monotony of the Central Meseta, though they probably wouldn't have been too keen on the torrential rain either. Yesterday, the weather was closing and now it has finally and irrevocably closed. We walk out into a heavy mist hanging over every peak as far as the eye can see, but somehow the village of La Faba still manages to retain the remote mountain magnetism that makes our hearts race. Paul and I love the atmosphere and dream vaguely of renovating something in one of those valleys, then hard common-sense kicks in. Renovation? Old barn with lots of character and a bread oven? We've just done that and we said Never Again.

When we go to collect the girls, Gwen's head is a murky smudge in the flying vapour, clearly alive. She gives me her morning bellow and I feel sick with relief. As we drop the electric tape, both horses rush past us and it is clear they have had a bad night, but not everything is bad, because the rain has washed away the previous day's sweat and soothed Gwen's back so that the swelling is barely visible. Lubie's intermittent bump has almost disappeared too. We tack them up and in spite of the weather I get the rush of euphoria that comes with getting back on the *Camino*. It doesn't last long.

The rain is freezing and has no respect for plastic capes, particularly the cheap ones made in China.

Within minutes we are paying for allowing 3-year-olds to sew on the poppers and mess up the hems. We are soaking wet and our extremities - hands, feet, noses and chins - are all numb with cold. Paul is right, if you see a vending machine wearing its plastic hat (we have seen three since coming into Galicia), you know you are entering a wet region. I'm trying to see the funny side of riding in the pouring rain, but it's just a tragedy, because the surrounding landscape would be beautiful and the track so carefully removed from the main road by the Galician authorities would be fully appreciated, if we could see them. Instead, we are surrounded by water in the air, on the ground and on every inch of our horses and ourselves. This is no fun and we resolve to get down the mountain as far as we can and then bale out.

Sixteen kilometres, and just when I am about to scream that I can't go on, the perfect *albergue* emerges out of the murk. I dismount, only to find that my legs have given up before the rest of me, so collapse as I hit the ground and fall so heavily I chip a tooth. It doesn't hurt, it's the indignity that upsets me, but the owner who has come out right on cue, pretends not to notice. 'Horses? Yes of course we can take them.'

If she had said 'you've won the lottery' I couldn't have been any happier. We are taken round to the back where there is a large barn with a series of stalls inside - just what the girls need after the previous uncomfortable night and today's soaking. Within seconds of getting them inside they have their noses plunged into their feed and then all we have to do is look after ourselves.

We take a double room with a bath and I am in heaven. This is probably one of the best and most environmentally sympathetic purpose-built *albergues* we have been in. The main building is in the traditional palloza shape, an elliptical construction with flat walls and a roof made of rye straw, but with all the modern comforts. I am as happy as the proverbial pig, and I can see from Paul's face that he is too. The only bad part is that we have had to leave Vasco in the barn with the girls.

After a hot shower we crash into bed and sleep for three hours. I haven't felt this tired for a long time, then again I haven't felt this cold for a long time either. We have just had a very necessary and painful reminder that we are well into September.

A communal dinner is served at eight and with clothes fresh out of the washing machine and dryer (unbelievable luxury), we are already feeling good, then it gets better. As we sit down at the long table we recognise just about every face, though we have not spoken to all of them. Nevertheless, there is a common feeling of having won through a very hard day and this is consolidated by our host the *hospitalero*.

Albergues can be rated in a variety of ways: the situation, the facilities, or the people who are in it on any particular night. An *albergue* can be an entirely functional place where people come to stay for a night and move on, or it can become enduringly memorable for the events and interaction that takes place there - some good, some bad. The individual ingredients are hard to identify precisely, but together they can create the perfect mix, and very often the *hospitalero* will have a key role. Tonight is a perfect example.

Dinner could have been a quiet exchange of pleasantries and the usual *Camino* talk about motives, self-discovery, farting and blisters. Everyone here has been on the *Camino* long enough to know it all off by heart, and even more embarrassingly to have occasionally contributed to it with gusto and conviction, but this time our Brazilian *hospitalero* has other plans and doesn't even let us get to our first glasses of wine, where the danger starts, before introducing himself.

Paulo tells us that he has been on the *Camino* and it has changed his life in a manner that could only be described as revolutionary. I feel a sigh coming on, but it is stopped mid-flow when he says he does not want to preach on this point. From here he quickly goes on to say that he just wants to know for himself and everyone else here, what being on the *Camino* has meant for each of us, truthfully, as opposed to what we imagine it should mean. Good so far. He hasn't asked us to try imagining ourselves or other people as vegetables. He hasn't delved into the worse-than-a-virus gigabyte of *Camino*-babble I downloaded before setting out and tried (honestly) to take seriously. He is just curious about what makes a pilgrim tick, and so am I.

We are asked to introduce ourselves, and in our own languages tell everyone around the table where we have started from and our experience. Five languages: French, Portuguese, Spanish, Polish and English. Seventeen people with seventeen different stories, all able to understand each other, because the theme is ultimately the same. Looking around the table, it is clear that no one here is a marching maniac and everyone has struggled. We have all had moments when being on the *Camino* has tested us to our limits, physically, mentally, with ourselves and other people, but we have got through because we are still here .... and isn't that bloody incredible! Just look at us, fat, old, young and unsuitable, stupid and incapable, only a handful of days away from Santiago de Compostela and the achievement of our various aims - it's not often you have so many successes staring you in the face on the same evening.

'And what about us then, Mr Chinn? As our executive manager and the only person with any sense in the team, what's your assessment of our performance?'

Paul's eyebrows raise and from the world-weary smile I know that I am not going to get my answer easily. I want to hear that we have done very well, especially me, because I have gone at least two days without a shower and peed into a hole full of flies, but Paul would not be Paul if he gave prizes away without a fight.

'Later.' I am told and here is what came later. I think it was worth waiting for.

PAUL

The space I expected to create in my head while spending all those hours in the saddle, was, for much of the early part of the journey, filled with lots and lots of practical stuff: simple survival on the rocky descents in L'Allier, watching for the first signs that Okapi will put the brakes on, the ever present boot check, searching and generally failing to spot where Vasco is walking and always trying to sense the mood of the horses and, of course, Babette.

Vertigo? Like Lubie, the more I become accustomed to the physical experience of being up there, the less freely the sweat flows. The daily focus on all the practical stuff had for a long time taken me away from the chasm of introspection into which I had expected my mind to fall, but as the going has become easier that spinning sensation has begun. Right now I have it under control. I just switch back into practical mode – worry about Lucy's preparation for Lycée, find a bank, search out some horse feed or sort the fittings on those boots – it's just like steering Lubie away from dark alleys. Of course this is what I have always done in life, so no wonder it is so easy. Creating too much space in my head and seeing too many possibilities is uncomfortable and confusing – so much simpler to think about the next thing to be done and put all my energy into it. After all it's not what you do it's the way that you do it - isn't it?

The *Camino* follows almost exactly an east-west path. Every morning, as we fall into our easy pace, I look at the shadow that Lubie and I cast on the white stone of the road ahead. The shadow has outline, but no texture or substance other than the road we tread, which lies directly in front of us. We step towards it, but never reach it, and yet by the end of the day it will be behind us, only visible to those close behind and leaving no mark on this one-thousand-year old road.

The shadow shows my pretentious hat, the pack that I have grown since saying farewell to Okapi and that stoop I have failed to eliminate since first climbing in the saddle. I daily ask whether this thing in front of me could be different and whether something more substantial would be left behind.

As I get this vertigo under control, I can from time to time let my mind fly and look down on the shadows painfully inching along the crumbling relic, while around them on the modern highways of France and Spain the other thousands swarm to their destinations in a fraction of the time. Some travelling North in the morning and South in the evening. Others following our path in the morning to travel eastwards as the sun sets. The only rule seems to be that they must go as fast as possible …. only to end up where they started.

From way up there you begin to see what people are doing to people and what people are doing to the planet, while the brashest newspaper headlines are invisible and the smartest politician spin inaudible. There are so many crazy things happening and yet the wax of my wings melts under the glaring realization that neither I nor any other pilgrim can make a worthwhile difference to a single one.

As we share dinner each evening with a different mix of pilgrims from a different mix of countries and the young Rioja encourages each of us to fly, we share the same sense of injustice in the world and the same feeling of powerlessness. Each of us searches to find that place in which we can do something, but I fear that despite our earnestness, as individuals we will each settle for inaction or such a small act that our shadows will fade without trace.

As I write here this evening I am afraid that the religions of the world have lost their way. Their flocks and their impact, preferring to concentrate on dogma and the issues of yesterday. I might hope for the spontaneous emergence of a personality that could harness international opinion and truly challenge the establishment (this is beginning to have Messiah overtones!), but this seems implausible and perhaps dangerous. I am therefore left with a sense that that the greatest impact that I could have is in proselytising and encouraging those with whom I have contact, to stand their moral ground and collaborate in resisting injustice.

Pigs with Wings

After a wonderfully warm and peaceful night in our bedroom we walk out into heavy rain, it's just like the day before and there doesn't seem to be any break on the horizon. I try to focus on the girls who have also spent a very comfortable night, but I am feeling bloody miserable. I hate feeling cold, I hate feeling wet, and feeling wet and cold at the same time is torture in its purest form. We slither out on to the slimy wet road and peer into the damp gloom. I want to go home.

An hour later the clouds suddenly start to thin out and I realise that we have been missing perhaps the most beautiful landscape yet. If they existed and weren't so terribly uncool, I would put an I love Galicia sticker on Gwen's rump. In fact, my gloom has already lifted, because the track has been really very pleasant to ride on. There have been some ascents and descents, but only enough to provide variety. We have also been through a series of what I can only describe as authentic farming villages; their houses hacked out of the local rock and the farms working as they must have done for centuries. Riding here is like a breath fresh air after nights spent in sweaty *albergues*, and if the sun had been shining I know we would have been yodelling euphorically. Still, at least the rain has stopped, it is marginally less cold, and because I am riding Gwen, I don't have to step in the liquidized cow poo when we walk through those ever-so authentic farmyards. I am happy and Paul is probably happier still, because he can see that I'm not in a bad mood any more.

We talk about getting to the end of the *Camino* and what that means and of course it means a great deal, but in our current mood we are content to agree that this is just the beginning of … something else.

Our final descent brings us into Sarria and the search for an *albergue* that takes horses, the usual process of despair and hope and despair ending in this isn't so bad after all-ness. Paul stops off at a tourist office and is told that the horses can stay in the local cattle market. We don't really know what this means, but it's somewhere they are allowed to stay, officially, and it's free so it's good enough for us. The other part of the deal is that we will be met there by the local police who have the key. Ideas of grandeur burst kaleidoscopically in front of my eyes. A police escort, a welcome committee, the local mayor coming out to tell us that travelling on horseback is getting back to the roots of *Camino*ship and then photos, photos, photos. Paul says – 'I think I've just seen a pig fly.'

In fact, it's not quite that exciting, though we are impressed by the service we receive. To date our angels have come in many shapes, sizes and clothes, but police uniforms are a first and if the Angel Gabriel had a body like theirs I'm surprised Mary behaved so well. Anyway, today it's the Flying Pigs who find our horses a home. A hundred cattle pens to choose from and no unpleasant neighbours. Within seconds of leading them through the door, Gwen and Lubie are in their element and up to their eyes in the bag of food someone has so kindly left behind. So, with the horses comfortably accommodated and the sun shining, almost, it's time to pause for a bit of eulogising. Are you ready? You'd better stand back because this going to be loud.

We love Galicia! In fact, it's so wonderful that when I'm rich and famous …. I'm going to buy it!

Galicia is probably most accurately described as a slightly sunnier Ireland or Cornwall. Inland, it oozes greenness from the high woodlands to the low, sheltered meadows and everywhere you look massive mountain ranges loom like a ring of protecting giants, helping the region and its people to keep their identity. In spite of this, Galicia has had its fair share of invasions – the Celts around 600BC, the Romans around 50AD, the Visigoths around 400AD, the Normans during the Middle Ages and the French in 1808. The region was also visited from time to time by Francis Drake in the 16th century. Interestingly though, it was largely unaffected by the occupation of Spain by the Moors from the 8th century onwards. True, the Arabs ransacked Santiago de Compostela in 977 and got a legendary beating round the head from St. James, but they didn't hang around much after that. Today's' latest influx of pilgrims is undoubtedly yet another invasion, though hopefully the strong Celtic influence with all the stroppy stubbornness that accompanies it, will keep Galicia, Galician. In fact, if I were a Galician politician I would pass a law to stop foreigners from buying property of any kind here. Furthermore, I would chuck out every foreigner forthwith, everyone that is, except me.

Still, the next day, even after all the nice things I have said about the place, it is freezing, and no one takes pity on us. Fine for you walkers down there, slogging up the hills and generating your own personal heat, but we poor riders, relying as we do on our horses to labour and sweat for us, are catching hypothermia. Then, gradually, the mist lifts to allow the sunshine through and we have a beautiful ride through mountainous countryside, patched with woodlands and small villages and once again we are completely charmed. Hey! What's this? Suddenly the *Camino* is full of new faces. In fact, we are in a continuous pilgrim jam, surrounded by pretenders, the one hundred kilometre wimps who go only this distance to ensure they get the certificate in Santiago. A coach drops off a large number at one point and we try to push on past them before they get going, but there is always another lot in front. On the way we pass Peter walking on his own.

'Where's Gabi?' I ask with all the tact of a rutting elephant.

'O she like go faster so she walks with some girls.'

Poor Peter, his poor little face says it all. Heidi has got pissed off with him and sent him back to his goats. Well, he is a bit of a Deutsche nerd, bless him. Maybe there are other fem-nerds on the *Camino* who will appreciate his special talents, though he'd better hurry because there isn't much further to go. I try to say something cheery, like the weather's better now, but Peter is plunged in a gloom that only our inspirational *Camino*-ist, Shirley Maclaine and one of her magic, orgasmic moments could pull him out of.

When we get to Portomarin we catch up with a Brazilian couple, Mate and Antonio, with whom we have shared a couple of piss-poor days before. I like them, because they moan about the weather as much as we do and let Vasco beg from the table. They are not hearty or hale weather and Antonio spends an hour every morning smearing cream into his feet to avoid blisters, a perfectly normal aversion to pain that I can understand. Better still, he does it in private and neither of them, as far as I am aware, have ever popped a blister or massaged each other inappropriately in public. My kind of people. We exchange addresses and hope to see each other further down the line.

Today we sleep in the tent, purgatory as far as I am concerned, though a little more exciting because our new one takes all of twenty minutes, as opposed to ten seconds, to erect. Paul and I manage this without arguing and the horses are given a good field. The charge six euros each, twice the price for a person in an *albergue,* someone here knows when they are on to a good thing. Still, we get our own back by emptying every apple tree on the site, for which our girls are very grateful and leave lots of fertile manure as a non-verbal expression of their thanks.

Portomarin, is a non-descript town, apart from three and a half factors that elevate it above the status of 'somewhere I went through on the way to Santiago de Compostela'.

The first is the fact that the real town was submerged under water in the 1960's, when the authorities wanted to build a dam and the inhabitants 'volunteered' to move out - compulsory purchase being another name for a kick in the groin and the threat to make a chorizo out of grandmother.

Second is the church of the Hospitallers, which was moved stone by stone and re-erected on a newly arcaded Plaza.

Third is Aimery Picaud's comment that "Prostitutes who go to meet pilgrims in wild places between Portomarin and Palas del Rei, should not only be excommunicated, but also stripped of everything and exposed, after having their noses cut off, to public blame." So maybe it wasn't the snoring that kept me awake, but why chop of their noses?

And the half? This, as Paul and I have agreed, is so closely linked to the third that it can only be taken as a fraction of the whole, which is too important to be overlooked. Perhaps there is something in the air between Portomarin and Palas del Rei, or perhaps we just can't see what is going on under our noses (ah noses!) all the time, but it is definitely to do with the libido. Lots of it and usually in the so-called mature man. Don't worry David, we are not using your real name, but you know who you are and you are in good company, crowds in fact, all lusting after the buxom pilgrim beauties half your age and in tight shorts. I suppose it is hard to resist, especially when the wife isn't there to see, but do you have to bring them to dinner and pretend that they are just good friends.

After our habitual pelegrino pasta, we move up a bar and meet Berndt, another German with whom we had spoken briefly outside Marcelino's bar a couple of days before. Not a very memorable conversation at the time, apart from his mention that he stayed in either a Parador or a good hotel every night. If he had told me this in the early weeks of our journey, I would have gone through the usual routine of denouncing the package holiday pilgrims, the ones who weren't prepared to really experience and understand the true hardships of *Camino* travelling, blah blah blah. The difference is that by now I have seen the light and know this blather for the hot wind it is. So I am pleased to see him and impressed when he tells me that he has done thirty kilometres that day. Good on you Berndt. We also find out that he is a retired super-chef, with a background in all the places where Paul and I only ever went on business expenses, while his wife is an haute-couture designer. Berndt stumps up a bottle of wine and too many brandies, so we sleep well in spite of having to use the horse blankets as mattresses.

Babette Gallard

Who left the heavenly hose on?

Today we are heading for Ventas de Naron and the *Camino* is running alongside the main road for a large part of the way, though it's not as bad as it could be because, once again, the Galician tourist board has done its utmost to ensure that the pilgrims are at least safe. Road signs warn motorists at crossing points and the *Camino* itself is put a good two metres in from the road.

Two hours in and the rain starts without even a warning shower. Someone in the sky turned on the hose and we are directly in the line of fire. We are miserable, cold and of course very, very wet. Vasco is shivering under my rain cape, refusing even to poke his head out when pilgrims who know us ask where he is, meaning that I have to lift the flap and get even wetter than I already am. The girls want to turn their bums to the wind, but we can't let them, because it is in the wrong direction. I know just how everyone is feeling and would catch a bus if a big enough one came along, but of course it doesn't so we have to press on, weaving our way in and out of the mass of one hundred kilometre pilgrims. I am not in a good mood and then Gwen finally decides that enough is enough, stopping in the middle of the road until Paul pushes Lubie in front, so now we are in no doubt that we have to find a place to shelter and soon.

Perhaps a half hour later we see a Hostel sign. A woman is standing at the door watching the rain fall in solid sheets. Paul shouts out to her that we are looking for two beds and a place for the horses, while I hold my breath and pray to whoever will listen that she says yes. She does and indicates a barn at the back.

Hell to heaven in the space of a second. The barn is big and draughty, but it is dry and the owner has hurriedly cleared a space in the general debris for the girls. We attach them to a large slurry tanker, opposite two other horses that are similarly attached. This is probably about as low as the girls have come in terms of accommodation. We drape the blankets over their backs and leave them to snuffle around in the mouldy hay they have been given. All fine, except for the dying cow in the corner. We try not to look, but its agony is clear. The poor beast has a huge growth on its side and when I go to the cow shed for water I see another, pitifully thin cow in a similar condition. As we walk back to arrange our own accommodation, Paul and I reflect on the inexplicable and in my view arbitrary attitude of the Spaniards to animals. How can people watch a bull slowly tortured to death, often fatally injuring the horses they are supposed to prize so much? Similarly, how can they fawn over our perrito, while their own dogs are tethered outside and lying in their own filth?

Enough of the negative. The owners of the hostel are the epitome of kindness, saying nothing as we and our disgustingly dirty dog drip our way into their pristine bar. We take the first table, hardly bothering to see who is sitting there, until he says hello. It is Berndt, also taking shelter from the storm and then Antonio and Mate walk in to complete the Santiago group. Like us they have decided to stop, because like us they hate the rain. We spend the rest of the afternoon and evening in the bar, steaming gently and watching with increasing horror the pictures of floods in the South of France and parts of Spain. Couldn't they have waited until we finished the *Camino*?

In the morning the hose is still running and the only good part is that the horses are inside and dry. I don't allow myself to im-

agine what condition they would have been in if we had only managed to get a field. We get up at seven thirty to a grey-black sky and ocean loads of water just waiting to dump on us. Antonio and Mate get up at much the same time and we regard each other with mutual misery.
This is going to be another piss-awful day.

'Never mind, Antonio says cheerily, 'I've got something that will help you.'

What? An umbrella the size of the sky may be? Or a truck to take us all the way to Santiago de Compostela without anyone else knowing? He holds out a tube of cream.

'O, great, what's it for?'

'People use it for babies when they have problems with the nappies.' Mate explains for him. 'Antonio uses it for his feet but it will be good for …'

'Our butts.'

With only three days left to go this kind of relief has come a bit late, but I'll use it anyway, because one pain less might make the day marginally more bearable.

The fine drizzle matures into pissing rain within seconds of us riding out of the barn. I am frozen and nothing Paul says can cheer me up, he tries once and then wisely stays behind with Lubie. The great shame of all this is that apart from some roadside riding, the rest is in forests on really good riding tracks. If the sun had been out we could have enjoyed ourselves, but it isn't and we don't.

Next, just to ensure that my mood is right at the bottom of the pit, we stop at a village only to be told that the *albergue* does not take horses and there are no others for six kilometres. I am beyond protest, I have lost the power of speech, my feet are too cold and my jaw is frozen over. We plod on and then see a couple we had met in France. A smile is required and I do my best, even when I don't want to talk to anybody. Then Vasco manages to make this the pissiest of all the piss-awful days on the *Camino*.

Vasco is usually compliant and fairly obedient, but like any living being he has a mind of his own. This becomes most obvious when he is enjoying running with the horses, does not want to ride and refuses to come to the stirrup to be picked up if there is a busy road ahead, meaning we have to get off. To avoid this, we have often asked people on the ground to do the work for us and to date it has worked well, because most of them know him and he knows them.

Today our acquaintance of the *Camino* is an unfamiliar face and Vasco is taken by surprise when he is picked up without warning. He has never bitten anyone ever before, he is the most placid and patient dog I have ever known, except that now he is scared and reacts in the only way he knows how. The bite is not a big bite, but it bleeds profusely. I am totally panic-stricken and don't know what to say or do. Fortunately, our friend appears to be quite sanguine about the incident and accepts responsibility. So what can we do other than ride on and feel very, very guilty. Where are you now St. James when we need you? A little miracle please, nothing on the scale of unhanging a hanged man like you did in Santo Domingo de la Calzade, just a quick stitch and a plaster, or better still a reversal in time so that it never happened at all. Perhaps I didn't pray hard enough or perhaps my stack of sins was already too high, but when we saw them two days later, our friends' hand had swollen like a melon, and his wife refused to speak to us.

In Melide, the town six kilometres on, life begins to look marginally less terrible. The rain gives us a break and we find the best *albergue* in the world – in the present circumstances. For the girls it has a couple of very basic stables where they are dry and warm, while for us it has a washing machine and a dryer. We throw everything in and huddle in our sleeping bags for the three hours it takes to make the clothes wearable again. Then we eat and while I call Lucy, Paul trawls the town for more oats and comes back with carrots. Meanwhile Gwen (the gossip) has her head stuck out into the small passage in front of her stable door, watching the hordes of people passing by and enjoying their attention. She could get into this new lifestyle. Best of all, the *hospitalero* has officially sanctioned Vasco's presence in the dormitory, meaning we do not need to bury him in our sleeping bag or smuggle him in our jumpers when we go out.

Why is it that the home stretch always seems the hardest? Just like the last screw, or the last day before going on holiday when you can guarantee the sky will fall on your head. First, we have the foul weather, and then we have the man who can snore from both ends. And guess what? In the morning it is still raining. We hang around and drink coffee in the hope that it will slacken, but it doesn't and we debate the possibilities:

Stay - no food for girls and risk of arriving late in Santiago de Compostela where Ray will be waiting for us.

Go – get wet and risk not finding anywhere with shelter for the girls.

O sod it, let's go. Either way it's going to be miserable, so what's the point of prolonging the agony.

The rain falls solidly for an hour and then we catch a glimpse of the sun and from there the blue gradually increases like a frame around it. Life is beginning to look up. In fact, we are almost dry by the time we arrive in Calle, a small village that a disgruntled pilgrim report on the web had identified as being pilgrim-unfriendly, though our experience couldn't be more different and we can only assume that he must have spoken to the wrong people. Calle is welcoming the pilgrim trade with bright-eyes and open purses. Fifty houses, two smart bars serving bocadillas at any hour of the day, and an enterprising woman who offers a room for us and a garden for our horses. When I try to warn her that our girls can reduce verdant spaces to moonscapes in less than half an hour, our host says it is not a problem and even repeats this half an hour later. Later, over a glass of beer, she laments the stupidity of everyone but the Spanish. The Americans for voting Bush back in, The English for letting Blair agree with Bush, and the French for having a French pilgrim naïve enough to try selling her donkey.

'What do we want another donkey for when we've got hundreds of the useless beasts already? And she wanted so much for it too. The whole village is still laughing.'

So be warned, future French and any other nationality of pilgrim with a donkey for sale. You won't even be able to give it away when you get to Santiago, and to my mind you shouldn't be thinking of it anyway.

Sunshine next morning and I like Spain again. Our last day on the *Camino*, I can't really believe it, and we ride on without even mentioning the fact, weaving in and out and up and down through eucalyptus woods dripping with moisture and cough-drop freshness. This is so much fun that I raise a smile for the hordes of one hundred kilometre pilgrims, and Gwen stops pretending to be a battering ram every time we meet a new group.

In Labacolla, or as Paul explains to me Lavacolla for the French speakers (laver: to wash, cul: buttocks), we consider following the old tradition of washing our bums in the Lavementula river before entering Santiago de Compostela, but one look at the water make us decide that it is a bad idea. Anyway it's all rather public and unnatural, particularly because someone has dumped an airport in the middle of the *Camino*, changing the atmosphere and adding at least another 5 kilometres to our journey. An ironic choice of location, when you consider that it is Santiago de Compostela's popularity with pilgrims and latterly tourists that made building an airport necessary in the first place.

Our next reminder that nothing is ever as simple as you think, is when we find out that the *albergue* strongly recommended by the nice *hospitalero* in Melide because it takes horses, does not.

'Orses? No we donnt take 'orses. This is a pilgrim hotel.'

'Well, do you know of any *albergue*s nearby that might.'

'I been 'ere since two weeks, how will I know zat?'

'So that means no.'

'Yes, it mean no and your 'orse he shit now.'

Why is it that since buying the pooper brush and dustpan, both Gwen and Lubie have lost the will to defecate on concrete, tarmac or polished marble flagstones, until now, when I am confronted by a congenitally unhelpful Frenchman. On second thoughts, if I wasn't so anally-retentive, I might do the same myself. Here's what I think of you and your pilgrim hotel. Now we have to find somewhere else for the girls and the only alternative our Frenchman can offer is a phone call to the police. I try first, but then Paul takes over because my Spanish is hopeless and I'm too angry to align my thoughts into a straight line of words in any language. Eventually, though I still don't know how he does it, Paul makes himself understood, and better still, is able to understand when he is told that the girls can stay in the new cattle market on the edge of the town.

We ride out, doing our best to stomp all over the patch of yellow stuff masquerading as grass. Unfortunately, in our fury, we forget to stop on the low, scrub-covered hill called Monte del Gozo, where, according to tradition, the first pilgrim in a crowd to see the city from the top of the hill was made king of the pilgrimage. He would later be called Leroy or Le Roy and could pass the name to his descendants. We had intended to dismount from our horses in respectful humility as they had, and may be take a few moments to clap ourselves on the back, instead we hit the dual carriageway at the bottom of the hill without even realising that we have passed all the good bits.

Actually, in spite of getting lost for half an hour, once we get to the cattle market it really isn't so bad. I mean, it's all modern and clean and there is hay and straw and a security guard. If there are any angels listening, then thanks guys. It may be a bit cavernous, and there is the drawback of having to move the horses out of the stalls tomorrow, because there is going to be some event or other, but they'll still be under cover and Ray is bringing two bags of feed later this evening so what's the problem? We tuck them up and quickly say goodbye, because next we have to find a bed for ourselves. Again it's all easy. We call a taxi and stop off at a central *albergue* where Vasco is allowed to stay in the entrance hall, while we are given three spare bunks for Paul, myself and Ray. Then we do what every pilgrim has to do, go stand in front of that massive cathedral, stare like goldfish and say 'we've done it.' Or something like that.

Babette Gallard

THANK YOU BERNARD

The master of stone who undertook the construction of the basilica of the blessed Saint James was called Bernard the Old – he was an inspired master.
Aimery Picaud

The Santiago Cathedral as we see it today is the result of a collection of building projects that started in the 9th century (when St. James's tomb was supposedly discovered and a small hut of stone and clay was built to shelter it) and finished in 1750 when the Galician architect Fernando de Casas y Novoa added a Baroque façade (the Obradoiro) on to the western side of the cathedral. In between these dates, churches had been built and destroyed literally over St. James's head, but his tomb remained intact, even when the Muslim chief, al-Mansur, took the church bells to Cordoba. In 1130 Aimery Picaud described a nearly completed cathedral, though unfortunately he was not able to see the truly breath-taking Portico of Glory that was only finished in 1188.

In the past, the vast majority of pilgrims came in from the north-east, passing the leper hospital, crossing the River Sar and finally entering by the Porto Francigena. As we walk today, I am determined to imagine how it must have been for them, after a journey so immeasurably harder than ours, but it's difficult to unimagine the ugly square concrete blocks the *Camino* wedges us between, or the shuddering thunder of buses and lorries shouldering their way through narrow alleys. In order to experience some element of their emotion, I must also forget the religious dishonesty behind the whole idea of St. James's relics being here in the cathedral, or whether in fact he ever came to Spain at all. I find it distasteful to think of how thousands of people over hundreds of years may have been and still are being duped, but when you stand in front of what is often described as one of the most beautiful medieval artefacts in all of Europe, the deception is almost forgivable. Even though I neither share the religion that motivated its construction, nor endorse the hardships this involved, I can't deny the sheer magnificence and scale of the building. A soaring structure pointing up to space and spinning the earth as I try to hold it in my own narrow sphere of vision. Paul and I are silent. We don't know what to say, because the whole experience has been about getting here, the journey, and now we are here. The sun sets as we leave, adding to the unreal, almost contrived sensation of the moment.

By now it is late, and Ray is obviously going to be even later, so we go out for a meal, a king-size meal to make up for all the pilgrim-size meals we've had before, washed down with buckets of wine. Well, we've made it haven't we? This deserves a celebration. After seventy-five days of riding, we, our horses and Vasco are here in Santiago de Compostela, a night away from riding up to the Cathedral and picking up our certificates. Great.

"Yeh, great … and er … what next?' It's my proverbial question. I can't help it. If I'm here I already want to be there. 'Jerusalem.'

'When? next year?'

'Yes, sort of. We could go via Rome, or may be North Africa, if Algeria has calmed down by then.'

I try to trace the route in my head, but geography has never been a strong point.

'Bit of a long way isn't it?"

'We can do it in sections, perhaps taking two years if we travel in the summer when Lucy is on holiday.
Have a think about it.'

'I've thought.'

'And?'

'Yes.'

It would have been a good note to end on, except that we haven't finished, and no one told us that the last kilometre of riding into Santiago de Compostela would be so hard.

Morning, and we think we are doing everything by the book. Phoning the police on a number as we have been told to by a member of staff at the pilgrim office the day before, and when there is no reply, stopping off at a police station on the way in. The problem is that it's a different set of police that deals with pilgrim business, and so we have try to phone again as we ride, probably breaking a law about using a phone while on horseback, and dodging buses as we go the wrong way up one way streets. We are turning into the pedestrian area when Paul finally gets. I know something has gone wrong when he turns purple. 'You're joking.' Pause, while he listens to the response and gnashes his teeth. 'It's impossible, we can't -' He is shouting by now and people are turning round to stare, some of them familiar pilgrims who have been cheering us in. This is not the way our brief moment of fame is supposed to be. 'Thank you, fifteen minutes. Yes, I understand.'

I breathe again as Paul explains that the police have told him that horses are only allowed to enter the Plaza do Obradoiro between eight and ten in the morning. It's now ten thirty, and permission has been granted on the condition that we only stay for fifteen minutes. A policeman posted outside the cathedral will tell us to go earlier if the horses are a problem in the crowd.

Problem? The girls are amazing. They tiptoe into the narrow alleys, avoiding the milling tourists and ignoring noisy fountains that would have sent other horses skittering like ballerinas on the booze. Perhaps they know it is a great moment. Vasco definitely senses something, because he is unusually restless on his seat on the pommel of my saddle. Then it's the steps. A flight of them into the Plaza that in our arrival euphoria we hadn't noticed yesterday. Are we going to be defeated at this very last stage?

'Abajo.' A man shouts to us and points to the right. Another way down, steeply sloping and treacherous for our girls in their iron shoes, but nothing is going to stop us now. We are going to enter that Plaza in style, on horseback, with our dog riding pillion. We look for Ray because he is our official photographer for the day. We want to make sure he catches the moment, every moment.

'Ray?'

Where is Ray? We scan the crowds and see the policeman who will chuck us out if there is any trouble. Mobs of people are coming towards us, wanting their pictures taken with our horses, but we still can't see Ray.

'Can I take your picture?'

How many times have we heard that on the *Camino* and smiled, even when it was the last thing we wanted? Now we want everyone to take our picture, a hundred times, and then send them all to us, because Ray is not here and he has our camera. We have to record the moment: our horses standing in front of Santiago de Compostela's cathedral with Vasco the feisty Foxish Terrier. I want everyone to know they did it.

Eventually, two people offer to email their pictures to us, meaning that Paul and I can relax and enjoy our brief moment of celebrity. We've missed Antonio and Mate, Berndt too by the looks of it, but Karin is there and the Norwegian woman who ate our inedible curry, and whose name we can't remember. Crapping Junior too, and hey that's the German who smiled at us all the time. So everything is fine, just fine, except that it's all over and now we have to slog all the way back up those one way streets and concrete alleys.

EPILOGUE

This is probably where the story should end, though of course no *Camino* pilgrimage really ends in Santiago de Compostela, or Finisterre, where we would have gone if we hadn't wanted to get back to Lucy as soon as possible. Don't worry, I'm not repeating that *Camino* mantra about going to Santiago de Compostela is hard, but coming back is even harder, it's just that I have got a few more details to add on, in case you think they have been forgotten.

If you want to know where Ray was. He was round the corner somewhere, probably a bar (though he denies it), just missing us. And if you think you know what we said when we met him again later that afternoon, it wasn't 'Where the fuck were you?' We had got a grip on ourselves by that time, and decided that we didn't need a photo to prove ourselves anyway.

We didn't go to the Mass either, but only because we were riding the girls back when it was in progress, and just the thought of that huge incense blower made me feel sick. Anyway, I probably would have done something pathetic like bursting into tears and using Paul's t-shirt to blow my nose on, before dropping my breakfast on the floor, so we agreed that missing Mass was fine. In fact, we spent the rest of the day just mooching round the town and indulging in some mutual back clapping with people we had met on the way. I won't bother to repeat what was said, because it has all been said before and it would be just too embarrassing anyway. Being on the *Camino* puts you on another planet for a while and you say the stupidest of things, but don't worry, everyone hits the earth with a massive bump when they go to get their pilgrim certificates.

NO EUPHORIA HERE PLEASE

If someone was Christian enough to put a sign over the doorway to warn unsuspecting pilgrims like us, the shock might not be quite so brutal, but as it is we are winded and hurt when a nineteen-year-old Generalissimo wannabe, pushes us out of the door and tells us to wait quietly on the stairs. Something Karin (who has just joined us) and I simply cannot do. Anyway, hang on a minute. There are people here who have battled their way over a thousand kilometres, and all right some, like that group of one hundred k-ers over there who haven't, but don't we all have the right to be a bit happy and a bit loud? Apparently not. We are just supposed to give these people our names and stand mutely while they fill out a piece of paper that looks about as exciting as one of my four, very average, O' level certificates, with some very suspect attempt to Latinise our names (Paul becomes Paulum)

'So what do you think of that then?

'I think we should go out and get very, very drunk.'

'Drunk and disorderly.'

'Absolutely.'

'What did you say?'

'Can't remember, because I'm disordern and drunkerly.'

'Oh good.'

'Why?'

'Because that makes two of us.'

'But there should be three of us.'

'Ray?'

Five minutes later and we would have missed the ten thirty Refugio curfew, even though it had been extended by half an hour to accommodate party pilgrims like us. How ironic, a night on the street after seventy-five on the road.

Our last day in Santiago de Compostela dawns and it is sunny, though for once I wish it wasn't. We stuff socks and sleeping bags into our rucksacks for the last time, not caring about the shampoo that is bound to leak, or the t-shirt I've probably left under the bed. Well it doesn't matter anymore does it? Then we drive over to the cattle market where we will load our girls into the trailer and finally go home.
Un-pilgrims, just ordinary people like everyone else.

The overflowing car park is a sign that something could be amiss, as is the cattle truck parked in front of our trailer. Then we turn the corner and are greeted by a massive, hot waft of cow dung. The whole hall is full of livestock. It's Friday. It's Market Day and our horses have turned into bulls with rings through their noses. What now?

We spot them, Lubie and Gwen jammed into a stall, with cows on one side and a group of pathetic ponies on another. Gwen's face says it all. 'So this is the thanks we get for all our hard work.'

It's so sad it's funny and when a big, beefy farmer asks me how much I want for her, I laugh in his face.

'She's got sixteen hundred kilometres on the clock. Why do you want to buy her?'

As the word goes round, the interest goes up, and soon we have

Riding the Milky Way

a crowd blocking our way out, almost too much for Lubie and Gwen to take, but not quite. They walk out calmly as if they were nearly sold at cattle markets every day, and climb up the ramp of the trailer like the old hands they really are.
Our wonderful horses and our amazing dog. Three *Camino* pilgrims, with two old idiots in tow.

We now had to adjust our conception of distance over again. A signpost that informed us we were five miles from a township had, when Jim and Millie supplied the power, also revealed that we would not reach that township for an hour. In a car, five miles was considered "there".
From These Are My People by Alan Marshall

It takes us just two days to drive home, travelling along the hated N120, in full view of the pilgrims who are seeing us now as we saw those cars only a few days before. Worlds apart. Did we really do that?
In this heat? Beep the horn Paul and I'll give them a wave. They won't know why, but we do.

A week after returning we ask our local vet, Monsieur Grellier, to give the girls a thorough check-over and make a more general comment on how they look after seventy-five days on the road. He pronounces them fit and well and gives us a certificate to prove it, though I still insist that Gwen would make a good advert for the RSPCA. Her hips stick out like a sick cow's, even when she is fat. We don't bother with a check-up for ourselves, but the bathroom scales say that I have lost five kilos and Paul three, while Vasco has actually got fatter on all the pilgrim-treats.

And finally ... a last word or two for Philippe and Alexandra: All right, so we admit it, we believe in angels. Not the Gabriel sort, with wings and an unflattering dress, but the sort that comes out to help you when you need it most. And on that basis I suppose anyone can be an angel, even me.

Our last camp-fire greyed to a mound of ash. Home to-morrow. No more yarns. No more messages.

Now it was over ... time to close my notebook, that link between them and me.

From These Are My People by Alan Marshall

Riding the Milky Way

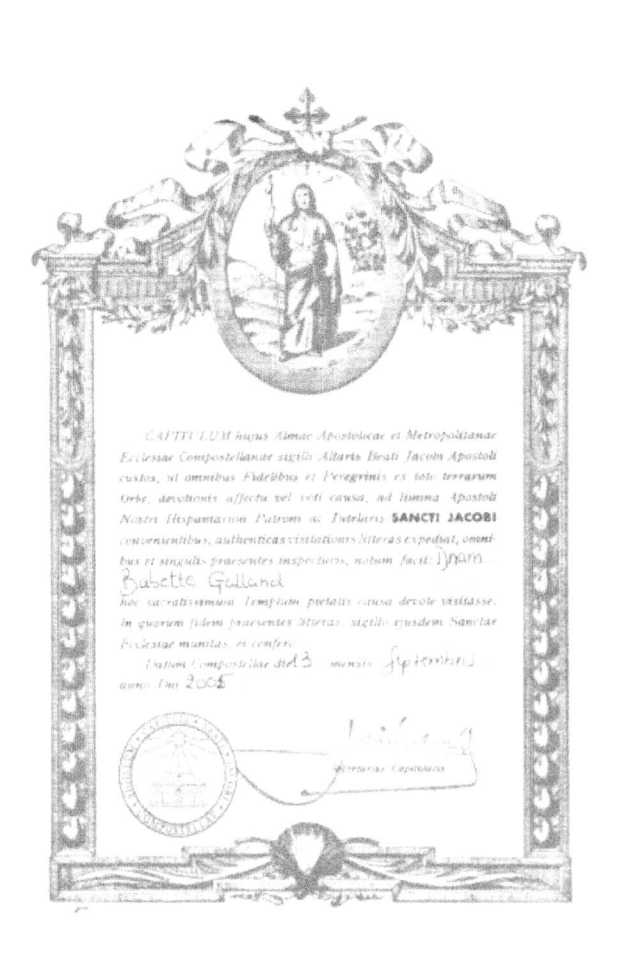

Babette Gallard

Veterinary letter certifying that the two horses are in good health (Note that Gwendolyn's real name, Krisma, is used).

Footnotes

As a result of our experience on the St. James Way in Spain, Paul and I have agreed that we will donate half of any profit we make from this book, to the financing of a poster campaign (run in partnership with the Spanish Tourist Board that will highlight the importance of keeping this ancient monument safe, clean and free of rubbish.

Finally, while we have neither the authority nor desire to tell future riders how to deal with their horses or donkeys, we hope that the following advice, gleaned from our own experience of making the mistakes, will be helpful.

ETIQUETTE

Long Riders must be responsible riders too!

On a number of occasions, usually in towns and more specifically outside restaurants and cafes, it was very clear that we and our horses were not welcome. This is a reaction that could be read in a number of ways, but our view is that the fault lies fairly and squarely with the riders and donkey walkers who went before us and did not take responsibility for the mess their animals left behind. If dog owners have to do it then so, do we.

PREPARATORY TRAINING

Don't even consider going on the St. James Way with your horse or donkey before you have ensured that:

He/she is one hundred percent traffic proof

He/she is familiar with crowds and generally noisy places

He/she can be tethered for a full night

He/she can deal with a variety of different feeds

Some people say your horse should be racing fit or at least extremely fit, for a trip like this. I tend to disagree. For me the most important aspect is that the horse/pony/donkey is carrying enough weight for it to be able to lose at least a quarter without becoming too thin. If not, you will either be forced to take a long break until the weight goes back on, or give up. Both horse and rider will become fitter by the day and as long as you can manage about 25 kilometres at the outset, you will do fine.

K IT

Rucksacks are a bad idea. Always opt for saddlebags, or better still if you can find someone to do it, organise a back-up team to carry your gear. This would also be a great help for finding and carrying food.

Buying cheap is often a false economy, so if you have the option, research the product, check that you are not being overcharged and then go for the best you can afford.

Throw out fifty percent of what you put in, preferably before you go. You will definitely find that you don't need it.

Don't carry a huge veterinary kit. A can of antiseptic spray, an anti-inflammatory gel or something similar, and (if you are allowed to) a course of antibiotics, is ample. The St. James Way is not in the North Pole and you can find vets and chemists along the route without any difficulty.

Saddle galls (with or without hornets) will probably be your biggest issue and we found that thick blankets are the best solution.

It's entirely up to you – but we found the bitless bridle that could also double up as a head collar, one of our best choices. Horses can make the most of whatever grass they can find and they are relaxed.

The Plastic Boots served us extremely well (for all the reasons already given) and we would not consider another trip like this using anything else.

Always carry a pooper scooper.

IDEAL TYPE OF HORSE

If you are thinking of riding the St. James Way, you probably already have a horse in mind, but my recommendation would be a stocky cob or pony, nothing over 15hh, and one can that maintain its weight. But as you can see we managed with two completely unsuitable horses and survived.

And finally ...

Listen to everyone, be prepared to take advice, read all the relevant literature but ultimately make your own decisions in the context of you, your horse and what you want to do. The rest is just hot wind.

An expert is one who knows more and more about less and less (Nicholas Murray Butler 1862 – 1947)

THE ITINERARY

Region	From	To	Kms
FRENCH SECTION Auvergne and Lozere	St. Polignac	Montbonnet	30
	Montbonnet	Monistrol d'Allier	14
	Monistrol d'Allier	Chanaleilles	72
	Chanaleilles	Aumont-Aubrac	30
	Aumont-Aubrac	Nasbinals	26
	Nasbinals	Saint-Chély-d'Aubrac	16
Averon, Lot, Tarn et Garonne	Saint-Chély-d'Aubrac	Espalion	24
	Espalion	Estaing	15
	Estaing	Conques	31
	Conques	Livinhac-le-Haut	26
	Livinhac-le-Haut	La Cassagnole	31
	La Cassagnole	Seuzac	30
	Seuzac	Varaire	26
	Varaire	Laburgade	23
	Laburgade	Lascabanes	30
	Lascabanes	Lauzerte	30
	Lauzerte	Moissac	23
	Moissac	St. Antoine	30
Midi-Pyrenees	St. Antoine	Lectoure	25
	Lectoure	Condom	28
	Condom	Eauze	28

259

	Eauze	Nogaro	26
	Nogaro	Aire-sur-l'Adour	30
	Aire-sur-l'Adour	Arzacq-Arrazigue	30

	Arzacq-Arrazigue	Arthez-de-Béarn	31
	Arthez-de-Béarn	Navarrenx	32
	Navarrenx	Aroue	18
	Aroue	Ostabat	25
	Ostabat	Honto	27
	Honto	Roncesvalles	29
SPANISH SECTION Navarre	Roncesvalles	Zubiri	22
	Zubiri	Villava	15
	Villava	Pamplona/Cizur Menor	10
	Pamplona/Cizur Menor	Villatuerta	37
	Villatuerta	Los Arcos	26
Rioja	Los Arcos	Torres del Rio	8
	Torres del Rio	Navarette	34
	Navarette	Najera	22
	Najera	Granon	22
	Granon	Villa Franca Montes de Oca	25
	Villa Franca Montes de Oca	Ages	16
Castile and Leon	Ages	Burgos	25
	Burgos	Sambol	25
	Sambol	Itero de la Vega	25
	Itero de la Vega	Carrion de los Condes	35
	Carrion de los Condes	San Nicolas del *Camino*	23
	San Nicolas del *Camino*	Calzadilla de los Hermanillos	22
	Calzadilla de los Hermanillos	Mansilla de las Mulas	24

	Mansilla de las Mulas	Leon	19
	Leon	Villadangos del Paramo	22
	Villadangos del Paramo	Hospital de Orbiga	12
	Hospital de Orbiga	Murias de Rechivaldo	21
	Murias de Rechivaldo	Rabanal del *Camino*	16
	Rabanal del *Camino*	Ponferrada	40
	Ponferrada	Villafranca del Bierzo	25
	Villafranca del Bierzo	La Faba	24
	La Faba	Fonfria	16
	Fonfria	Sarria	24
	Sarria	Portomarino	22
	Portomarino	Ventas de Naron	13
	Ventas de Naron	Melide	27
	Melide	Calle	23
	Calle	Santiago	31
			1587

[1] A small saddle horse, hardy and a good carrier.

[2] A breed most commonly associated with the area of La Perche, a district of Normandy, France. A large, strong horse primarily used for riding and light draft work.

[3] Leather over-trousers.

[4] Designated and well signed walks.

[5] St James Way

[6] Serving basically the same purpose as the crupper, except that it passes across the chest of the horse to prevent the saddle from slipping back.

[7] A strap of leather fastened to the saddle and passing under the horse's tail to keep the saddle in place

[8] A girth or strap for holding on a saddle, rug or anything else that is designed to remain fixed to the horse's back.

[9] Basically – in the wilds

[10] Guest house

[11] dovecote

[12] A serious and painful disease of the foot in equines – usually due to carbohydrate overload.

[13] Road or way.

[14] The horse pivots on the inside front leg.

[15] Hostel.

[16] Between the fetlock joint (best compared to an ankle on humans) and the hoof on a horse.

[17] The equivalent to a gite d'etape in France or the closest thing to a youth hostel in England.

[18] Wine store.

[19] Hospitalero/a - The warden, usually voluntary, of an *albergue* in Spain.

[20] High, steppe-like plains where sheep and wheat are the main sources of wealth.

[21] Snack sandwich consisting of rock hard bread with an omelette/tortilla filling.

[22] Equestrian Centre in Spain

Printed in Great Britain
by Amazon